In the Name of
Allah, the Merciful, the Compassionate

The Protector, and The Eternal. I ask, help and strength to be able to finish this project. I ask, Guidance and Blesings in the Name of Muhammad e Mustafa (the blessing for the entire mankind) saw and Lastly, I ask for Wisdom and Forgiveness for all I am about to interpret and all the unintentional mistakes I might make in the process.

Oh, Allah makes this a Sadqa Jaria for me and a source of guidance and blessing for all those reading and going on a journey with me through the mean of this book.

May Allah protect me from being a hypocrite and someone who preaches something he does not practice himself.

THE CERTAIN

IN

UNCERTAIN

BY

Muhammad Billal Ali

ISBN: 9798693407091

Price: 9.99

International variant

In collaboration with Amzon, hope you enjoy it. Cannot wait for your reviews!!

DEDICATED TO

The mercy for the entire universe, the soul of the existence, One of the bright lights of the creator, the purifier of the heart, the pearls of the eyes, and the shadow of love. The most magnificent among the creatures, to whom beats thousands of hearts for. O the White Moon rose over us, from the valley of Wadā', and we owe it to show gratefulness, where the call is to Allah! O you who were raised amongst us, coming with a word to be obeyed, you have brought to this city nobleness. Welcome the best caller to God's way!

I dedicate this book to my Leader, my Guidance, and my beloved Imam of all Prophets Muhammad Ur Rasool Allah (saw)

Here are some of **my favorite sayings**, of The Dignified Muhammad (S.A.W)

"A believer is not bitten twice from the same hole." (A believer is not mistaken twice with the same fault)".

"Those who cheat are not of us."

CONTEXT

ACKNOWLEDGEMENT

Honored and glad to be blessed with an opportunity to acknowledge the people who hold great value in my life. Never truly had a chance to acknowledge all these very important people in my life. Never been a high achiever or even an achiever, but to everyone who ever believed in me, THANK YOU.

Starting off with my late and great grandfather. Not just the grandfather but my spiritual master. Someone who taught me more about life and spirituality, after passing away then in real life. Thank You for guiding me always.

Cannot appreciate my fighter of a dad enough, your love made me grow. From making midnight snacks to fulfilling very unreasonable wishes. I only pray to be as capable to be called your son. Thank you for the selfless love you gave. This one's for you ❤

My ultimate supporter, a true inspiration, and one hell of a person, my mother. Someone who no matter how much be disappointed at me always encouraged me. I hope you like this surprise.

My two weird but awesome brothers Taha and Tallal. The ever expressive and the hardworking. You both are nice people. May Allah bless you both. (Oh, happy married life to you, Taha!)

And my beautiful grannies, you both the cutest My Allah SWT bless you both with a healthy and peaceful life ahead.

I would like to especially thank Izaan Ishaq and Arham Anwaar for helping me in the book.

The First Ever Book Review

The cover is sometimes everything, here it's the same, the title of the book is so catchy, really deep and philosophical which forces me to read the book and to know what could be "certain in uncertain". Even without reading the book my mind took me in various directions and encouraged a spirit of combating personal emotions in a direction that could help me manage uncertainty created by unexpectancy.

The book is written by a teenager which is one of its kind. The boy has a good grip on social subjects at a very young age. He is a Certified Life Coach, helping youth in understanding life and the worth of perspective and mindset in this materialistic world.

Book carries guiding principles of DESIGN THINKING & RELATIONSHIP MANAGEMENT with the flair of many interrelated subjects. Written in a very simple English, a lighter tone and language with a combination of slangs to engage the youth and to build their understanding on the subject. The book engages all ages and group levels and is helpful for everyone, if read with an open mind.

The writer emphasizes to stay away from Negative emotions and to cultivate the Positive one by feeding the positive only to help making the same life a paradise. The concept, always advised by WISE MEN from all eras.

The beauty of this book is the normal life examples, true expressions, simple yet mature. Indicates that the writer has good research on prevailing social issues, the mindset, the reaction and he has suggested some solutions from his own experiences. We should encourage the new writer by appreciating him on managing expressions and issues so well and in an understanding manner which can help both seniors and youth to tailor them according to some suggested guidelines.

The blend of modern science and spiritual inclination adds the uniqueness and beauty of the scripted document.

The writer needs to be a little more diverse and we expect that his next piece of art will surely cover that diversity.

The book is must read to understand how youth feels and to bridge the generation gaps also it would help the social scientist to understand how the youth can be engaged to carry along without heavy challenges. As well as massive inspiration and ideas for the youth to express on."

Samera Shaikh (aka Ummy aka Mommy)

Human Resource and Management Guru

INTRODUCTION

In the Name of Allah, The Most Gracious and The most merciful. The Creator, The Protector, and The Eternal. I ask, help and strength to be able to finish this project. I ask, Guidance and Blessings in the Name of Muhammad e Mustafa (the blessing for the entire mankind) P.BU.H and I ask for Wisdom and Forgiveness for all I am about to interpret and all the unintentional mistakes I might make in the process.

We live in one of the most uncertain times as a community, individually and as the whole human race. We live in a world where we are controlled by more strings than ever before. Whether it may be, Social media, our emotions, our relationships, or even our insecurities. In this book, I will be touching every aspect of our life directly and indirectly that controls us, and find answers in pursuit of finding consciousness in our lives. Through consciousness and control, we put forward the idea of a certain lifestyle.

"Control your desire or something else will"

A book connecting two very different ideologies into one very detailed perspective. On how to be ready to face any challenges and opportunities sent by life and have the peace of mind and control of the self to ace them.

Let's dive into the name a little, what is certainty? A state of composure, positivity and patience. Uncertainty, an obstacle, tough patch or situation. Certainty is a way of living, likewise Uncertainty further comes in three major aspects, 1. Uncertainty in Relationships (Community Oppression, Breakups) 2. Uncertainty in Mindset (Perspective, Fears, Insecurity) 3. Uncertainty in Spirituality (Anxiety, Desire, Discomfort) in the book, we would bring forward the idea of certain lifestyle, what it is and how to achieve it. While discussing all the topics and their byproducts in detail. Also featuring some practical exercises and ways to grow your state of certainty. The book is written in a way, it will help you understand, distinguish and grow the mindset, with thoughts and practices that will eventually lead you to a life in which you have the control of the self.

This isn't just a "book" it's your partner on a journey of self-evaluation and reflection. Together, we find answers, we find reasons and we evolve the mindset. In order to achieve certainty and control, on a road to find your purpose and consciousness.

DISCLAIMER

The following book can seriously trigger your ego, emotions, and most importantly your mindset. So, I would suggest you enter the book by leaving your ego and desire to prove me wrong outside. By the end of this book, you might want to change a few things around the mindset. This book will surely make you think a lot.

I welcome you in with an open mind and will to learn and grow. The purpose of any book is not to bring you an infinite amount of knowledge. But to make you think and help you bring more perspective to life.

In the following book, we will dive deep into the topics and subjects that are relatable and hold great value in our lives. And how we can come to the point of certainty while managing our resources efficiently.

The book is intentionally written in a soft easy tone with only one purpose to provide value and growth to the reader in whatever way I can. I tired to be as unbiased as possibles but yet I was very candid with my religious perspective.

be as unbiased as possibles but yet I was very candid with my religious perspective.

UNIT #1

AMPLIFYING THE SELF

Homosapiens, a creature came to existence almost 200,000 years ago. Also, known as the most superior among the creatures. A social animal with immense power to think and question, but likewise surrounded and doomed in its own will.

"In the illusion, is lost a gem trying to become the better metal"

Through the next few hours, we will be talking about human behaviors, emotions, and mindsets. As humans, we go through various emotions, situations, and struggles throughout our lives. Regardless of our age, gender, and social class. Emotions are something that makes us beautiful, vulnerable, and fragile. Unknowing of the future, functioned to make blunders, having no control over our behaviors can make life very hard to live. In this book, I will try to present you with a perspective, no matter how uncertain life is and can be, with proper channeling and maneuvering our resources. We can come to a point in our uncertain lives where we have some certainty that could give us a greater edge in achieving our goals and living a healthy, peaceful, and purposeful life.

CHAPTER #1

EMOTIONS

---

motions are the feelings you live, without Eemotions a person's life is like, a beautiful valley located in between the mountains surrounded by lush green outfield but it's empty. The light of the mind and the expression of the soul. It's the phenomena that keep you moving day after day, the feeling of empathy, compassion, and joy. If you wouldn't feel guilty for doing fraud with somebody, if you don't feel empathy for fellow human beings or if you don't feel compassion for your love and enthusiasm for your passion. Do you think you would ever be able to survive? And even if you did, do you actually think there would be any such thing as purpose? Just like robots or the angels from the heavens you would be just following the orders. But that's not what you are, you are a creature who can go rebellious, who can think and who can choose.

Thus why always remember, even the smallest of

the rocks and the heaviest of the mountains everything is created for a motive, with a purpose and by The best of planners. We as humans are born very ambitious, anxious, and short-sighted. Born pure, **we grow into the impurities of our society, traditions**, and enslave ourselves to our own desires. Born from a drop of the unpleasant fluid, we grow into egos larger than castles and taller than the sky. The most compassionate yet the most vicious creature in the universe. It's safe to say, humans are the most bizarre living entities out there.

Emotions just like humans can be difficult to understand, but we all face difficulties encountering them, accepting them. "The fun thing about your emotions and mind is, there isn't any **guide manual** to it". Unlike a cure to cancer or heart stroke there isn't a right or wrong answer to your emotions, but yourself. As patterns and behaviors change, knowing no two brains are the same. You deal with your emotions and you regulate them rather than them controlling you. Because if you enslaved yourself to your emotions, which by the way is a very common phenomenon. People tend to go by how they feel, although they do not understand feeling is a complex set of behaviors that are unpredictable and uncertain. Thus, in order to be certain in uncertainty, we need to take back our control over our emotions, so that we can free ourselves from the infinite desires of "breaks, moods, and burnouts". There isn't much we can control, from the external factors, affecting our lives but do understand you are the sailor of your ship.

In this chapter, we will be specifically talking about various emotions, why we get stuck in them, and how to take conscious control over your feelings. Oh, by the way by control I do not mean how we fake a smile or control our tears. But to genuinely, from the inside keep yourself at peace and spread positive vibes.

The self-control I will be talking about can also be found in ancient Greek philosophy in around 300 BC, the will to control destructive or intense emotions is defined as Stoicism. Stoicism is a topic in itself that I would not be opening up much.

While being aware of the struggle, we all face mood swings, depression, lack of "happiness" and the need for breaks/ escape. I am here to put forward the idea of emotional stability and control.

Emotions more than the situation depends on how

we carter them. What you feel is a byproduct of how you think and evaluate your situation. As human beings, it's our subconscious behavior to react to everything going wrong in our lives. Have you ever felt appreciative of the approximately twenty breaths you take in less than a minute? I am not talking about the feeling of realization or guilt, which we face after coming across these facts. I am talking about, like how you feel sad, do you ever feel grateful sometimes?

Have you ever tweeted?

"Ah, I am feeling too grateful today, thank God".

Feeling grateful with 78 others?

The matter of the fact is, we as humans are born ungrateful and ungracious. Not only that, but we also get to forget everything going right in our lives. Because we perceive that as a <u>regulation</u>. The control I am talking about starts with the small yet super effective changes we need to make in our behaviors and mindset.

There are mainly two types of emotions a person faces. The mainstream and their byproducts. For example, Happiness, Sadness can be defined as the byproducts of emotions and feelings, like pain and joy.

There are other types of emotions interrelated with your insecurities such as Jealousy, hate, etc. (Will discuss them in the next chapters)

Emotions are, **"An emotion is a complex psychological state that involves three distinct components: a subjective experience, a physiological response, and a behavioral or expressive response.**

The primary emotions a person feels, anticipate, and fear the most, with happiness being the crush and sweetheart of the masses, sadness on the other hand, is the "phupho ka beta"

Now I know, a lot of us have trouble finding happiness and overcoming the dark days in our lives.

Let's start with the crush of the masses,

Happiness.

"Happiness is perishable" and happiness needs a reason to revive itself. Whereas what you truly want your life to be is, peaceful and at ease with nothing going abnormally wrong. As I said in one of my podcasts,

"The youth looking for peace, running behind satisfaction and calling it happiness"

Let me put happiness into perspective, we are brought up with this presumption in our heads, that with achieving that or with buying that, whether it be a car, or the first position or even a dream girl. We would become "happy". Not only becoming happy, but we would also stay happy. Although happiness is subjective, no one or nothing can "keep" you happy. Stop depending on uncertain things or people to bring you happiness, as that eventually takes you so away from the purpose of emotional stability.

Likewise, happiness can never be a goal. Because you just can never achieve it all at once, it's like a constant cycle that cannot be persevered. The reason why I am emphasizing on happiness so much is because of how vulnerable and greedy we are to this emotion. Now don't get me wrong, happiness is a blessing and it feels great to be happy.

But the truth is, the life of this world doesn't revolve anywhere near the idea of happiness. Look at it objectively the world is anxious, greedy, selfish, and careless. Are you sure you are looking for happiness in the right place? Also are you sure you can STAY HAPPY at such a materialistic and selfish place?

Well, the clear answer is no you cannot, why because simply this is not how this world is functioned to be, and yes, I believe your happiness is affected by your surroundings and situations. As you just can't stay happy if your loved one is in pain, you just cannot stay happy when your community is under oppression. But you can stay positive and patient.

"Happiness isn't a result, byproduct, or a goal. Happiness is just a feeling and an expression of relief after a tough period of time"

One of the biggest reasons why we are filled with dissatisfaction and disappointments in our lives is because of the fact we perceive wrong not stopping there, we then make presumptions and start believing them. This world isn't the happy, fun wonderland you are expecting it to be, life bends the biggest and the bravest to the knees. Stop expecting, start adapting. We will only grow into our own misery if we do not adapt as soon as possible to the fact that happiness is rare,

It is the break between the innings not the end of the match.

People cheat on their long and healthy relationships in order to satisfy their presumptions about happiness. People do all sorts of wrong just to get fame or money as they think they will become happy after having those.

"In order to have a positive and peaceful life, you do not need happiness, wealth, or even health. Just the realization of all the things going right in your life"

The problem here is, we have been fed throughout our lives that we would be either Happy, excited, delightful or we would be Sad, depressed, and anxious. And what I am simply, trying to tell you is, if you want consciousness in life you do not need, happiness or sadness.

It's fine to be none, in fact, a person most of his life is at the baseline of emotions or what you call autopilot, survival mode. There's a reason, I was preaching peace. As peace is a mental place, above the baseline, and below the happiness. The good thing about peace is your mind is calm and positive. Unlike in happiness, your neurons are not hyperactive and charged, nor like sadness, low and negative. The best thing about peace is, **it's lasting**.

Peace can be in a way a synonym of "happiness" like how we say, "May you have a happy life", that doesn't necessarily mean an ever-exciting, charged life. But a life in which you are at peace and ease.

Similarly, when someone is at peace, their mind and soul are free of unnecessary burdens, anxieties, breakdowns, and discomfort. Which itself creates more positive thoughts, which eventually can **lead to happiness**.

So do not chase happiness, nor hide or be afraid of sadness. Try being at peace, as emotions are reasoning of your thoughts and uncertainty of your mind, so when your mind is positive and soul at peace. You would be in a solid place, ready to face your fate graciously.

Sadness

Sadness is like that one teacher of the class, which gives the most genuine lessons but because of her way the whole class hates her. **"Sadness is underrated"** to begin with, I know sitting on my couch writing all this is easy, I know the feeling of grief is interrelated to pain and sorrow. And we as humans have different levels of conceding and bearing of pain. So, trust me, I am not generalizing the feelings you feel or the emotions you go through. But also, believe me when I tell you, the pain you feel and the pain you go through is in relation to the levels of patience you have bottled inside you.

"Allah does not burden a soul beyond that it can bear" (02:286)

All power and respect to everyone in any sort of spiritual, physical, mental, or financial pain and hardships,

"Indeed with hardships comes ease" (15:85)

Now as I quoted the Ayah here, coming back to the first Ayah. One thing you need to observe deeply there is, "Allah does not...." which to make it simpler means all the burden you add to yourself, all the unnecessary pain you add to yourself is just not counted here. Allah tests a person by,

"Surely we will test you, something of fear, hunger and a loss of wealth, lives and fruits" [Baqarah]

And if we get deep into all the categories, we cover almost all the major aspects of pain and sorrow. Other than the part, in which due to our self-pity, assumptions, and expectations we get constantly hurt, over and over again. Stuck in a loophole of sorrow, just because of the added pressure and burden we put on ourselves. Similarly, it's not necessary if you go through a test, you become sad or depressed. As the great Ali bin Abi

Talib (a) rightly said:

"A momin has the same mood in tragedies as they have in comfort"

Understand this point, Allah tests you but that's it. Now how you react to it is all on you. For example, I bought a luxurious car with all my life's work, and boom it gets struck by a tree. Now, this is a test, how I react to that moment is all on me.

Similarly, there would always be divine wisdom to that crash, but we wouldn't be able to see it. Usually we aren't able to find out the wisdom, **up until our wounds heal up to the level our eyes start to open.**

Now, I do know one thing for a fact, that there is no such thing as an "easier pain" there are no comparisons in what a person feels, what might be easy for you can be a living hell for the other person. And as a Life Coach and someone who is entrusted by people as they feel comfortable sharing themselves with me. One of the things I am most vigilant about is to not judge or assume their pain even if I have experienced a similar or even the same incidence in my life.

Pain is hard, it's a part of a process. We go

through several types of pains in our lives. But if you especially, in emotional pain for ages you need to know.

Pain is like a drug, it's addictive. It gives a weird reverse psychological pleasure to the mind and soul. It is like the nicotine of emotions, we know it's bad but we have a weird guilty pleasure connected with it. It's not like we cannot control it, it's obviously not easy, But not impossible either. But let's be honest here, we love vibing through this unorthodox pleasure, whether it may be through tweeting about it, or listening to specific melodies to reactivate it again and again. It makes us feel heard, it makes us feel relatable and somewhat unique, how often you hear this phrase "no one understands me" or "there is too much on my plate" in our heads it becomes an excuse for us, for not doing well in any of the practical aspects of life. Ever wondered how everyone wants to be this mixture of Bill Gates, Nelson Mandela, and Steven Hawking but are not willing to put in the right amount of effort and energy, it is because we as humans love to look at the bright sunshine but hesitate and procrastinate to work for it.

Again, I am not here to pass judgments about

anyone's pain or suffering but look at it from this angle, **as long as the tap is left slightly open, the water will keep on coming out. No matter how many towels you put at the bottom to absorb it"**

I have gotten a few texts, with different respected stories and situations but they all came to a point where the person goes like "I try, I genuinely try but I cannot stop myself from thinking about that person or that event of my life.

now, the solution to your problem hangs not in you forcing to literally shut off a whole emotion of your body, but to simply turn off the tap by facing it, now facing can be of any type with respect to your situation but there will always be a way to facing your pains, accepting them and moving on.

Being aware of why something bothers you is the first step in overcoming it. Now, I know, we all struggle with our past, we all have some memories we get stuck into, we all face difficult times in our life. We all have and we all will continue facing a difficult time, it's never the bad event or misfortune in our life that causes depression. It's our impotence as human beings to move on and grow from the situations, which eventually leads to them being piled up. And with every new hardship, it becomes harder and harder the pain and anxiety to bear and live with.

"Facing difficult situations is regulation, staying sad is a choice"

Similarly, I was once having a talk with my cousin. He said something very bizarre that struck me really hard. So I was talking to him about hardships and pains, and how they vary from people to people and person to person. With respect to their strength and conditioning. Anyhow, he said **"If we as humans didn't had the instinct to move on, one funeral in a family would have been the reason of the whole family dying"**

That struck me really hard, I started to observe a little more in-depth. On why we are depressed so much, in order to diagnose that I jumped in how we get depressed.

Depression is a state of fatigue that causes hopelessness and disbelief, among the self. Some of the major reasons for depression can be the loss of something or someone, dealing with a failure, or static life patterns.

All of these are the byproducts of overthinking, self-victimization and self-pity. All of this further happens because of the negativity of the mind and the disability to move on.

The reality is we are not ready to let go of the past, as unsatisfying as that may sound. We are afraid of change and the thought of moving on isn't the easiest. We feel threatened and insecure about knowing the fact, the past didn't go well for us and what if it may happen again, or worse. We get stuck at that moment, failing to adapt to the change. Feeling pity for what happened and why it happened and "how it always happens to us" rather learning from the past, for a prosper future.

Let me give you a more technical perspective, and let me take the most relatable example of betrayal. Now the things that actually put you in that bad position, after obviously, the early few days of shock and denial. Isn't the event that happened to you, but rather **why it happened to you** and **how it always happens to you**? You see the pattern? You see how your mind actually makes you the victim and adds more fuel to your burning coals.

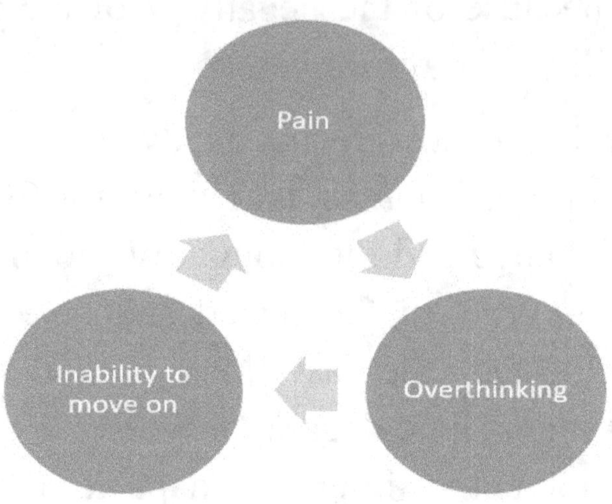

The Grief Loop

Moving on doesn't mean you forget those events or you somehow with a magical wand erase the memory. It means to just accept the fact, ease the mind, and the go-ahead to the next journey, level, or situation in life. Ever wondered why some people take revenge? Well, they do it to achieve peace with the past that was haunting them. That being said, for me it was always the forgiving that helped. **"As forgiving is the most respectable of revenge"**

Now that we discussed why we "stay sad". Let me share one of the very hard and personal times of my life with you, in order to inspire you and make you understand what I mean by controlling your emotions. Not a long ago my beloved father was diagnosed with cancer, he went through a very critical and intense surgery which was successful with the blessings of Allah. But it was a very detailed surgery with many risks and postoperative complications, so we had to stay there for a couple of weeks, most of the time we used to stay in the hospital for days, as in for complete twenty-four hours in the hospital environment, when the Covid-19 situation was at peak. Now you know, how stressful, anxious, and depressing the hospital environment can be. Staying there for days consecutively and for the reason I was there in the first place. The silence, the atmosphere, the lack of air and comfort was suffocating me emotionally. You can understand the anxiety and tension, I might be having at that time, but I told myself something.

" Billal, you should understand the fact that you are going through a test of resilience and patience. Now is not the right time to feel your emotions, express your emotions, or even to let them grow. Understand why you are here, in the first place. To cry? To be sad? And pass negative energies? Why are you here? You are here because your family needs you. They need you, don't put unnecessary pressure on them. It's

hard for all of us, but you have no reason to be scared or be sad because you have a power greater than any other which is trust in the Almighty.

You know the funny thing was, just because I showed no emotions or rather contained emotions. Many believed, maybe I was not as affected by all of this or I am just the least bothered. Anyhow, my emotions were as real as anything, I was hurt, and I was in pain, MY DAD WAS THE PATIENT!!

But I controlled my emotions because I had people to morally and practically support. This story of mine is not only an inspiration for you my friend. But an answer, that yes, you can control your emotions. I will again repeat, by controlling my emotions I do not mean to stop the tears or to fake a smile. But to genuinely, from the inside keep myself at peace and spread positive vibes. It's not like it was a one-time thing, every single moment when I used to be alone or tensed by some news, my anxiety used to creep in, the silence used to spread. It's like, I just didn't open the path, I didn't let it grow, I didn't let it settle in. And I was successful in not letting my emotions get the better out of me, in fact, was able to share strength with my loved ones

Similarly, once the factory of a 67 old man, caught fire. The fire was so massive that it burnt the old man's lifetime work in a few hours. Now the old man could've been sad, angry, depressed. He could've been like "why all this always happens to me?", "why can't I just be happy?". Do you know how he reacted? He asked the people around him to bring their families as they would never have seen such a massive fire show. That old man was Thomas Edison. And the very next year he made 10 million dollars of the same business. Edison wasn't dumb or "emotionless". He was just smart enough to know, playing the victim mindset or panicking wouldn't make anything better.

There's a lot you can learn from these stories but most importantly. The conscious art of living in the moment and adapting to the situation, rather than practicing your emotions.

"You only gain control when you reject to imprison yourself to your emotions, desires, and moods"

Victim Mindset

Never be so consumed and enslaved to your emotions that you lose your power to see, think, and process. Never let your "depression" , your pain or your negativity become the eyes you see from and the mind you think from, because my friend, I see this all the time, this is what we call the victim mindset. When all we see is pain, all we think about is negative thoughts and assumptions and all we observe is injustice and deprivation. We feel pity for ourselves, we feel less, our mind makes us feel lonely and that no one apparently "loves" us. Ever thought why? Like for example, if yesterday my brother would have been rude to me and my mother supported him supposedly. I would not like that, I would go to my own room. You see its all okay till here. You know when does the thing go absurd? When we start to fuel our negativity and feed ourselves assumptions through the victim mindset. It's a loop, most of us are stuck in. Because life is that way, there would be moments which you disagree too, but through this mindset, we literally look for excuses to be sad and need proper reasons to be "happy". And these set of thoughts, that no one loves me, no one understands, no one stays with me. They all are nothing but LSD for your mind. I know your situation would be hard, I know your past might not be the greatest. But I do also know, your mindset needs to be changed. How to change it? Well, you simply need to dig down deep inside your mindset and awaken a new voice of gratitude inside the head. Secondly, you ADMIT to yourself, with all honesty, the life of this world isn't meant to be happy and relaxing. It's supposed to be hard and difficult to your highest levels. But that doesn't take away the fact, you are able to breathe, your digestive system is working fine. And a sharp sow cuts the tree faster, all these hard times leave you with resilience and wisdom. Life isn't going so wrong, just as yet. As I said earlier **we are obsessed with finding wrongs in our lives** and feel bad for them. Thirdly, constantly feed yourself, you are good enough, awaken this instinct inside your head that constantly gives you positive reasoning to the unreasonable and manipulated thoughts of self-pity and victimization. In fact, constantly forcefully feeds yourself positivity. No matter how much your mind pukes it. Always keep on feeding it, to eventually change the pattern.

A Deeper Perception

So a few days ago, I was playing regular cricket with my neighborhood friends, and while bowling, I got hit by the ball trying to catch it. And I accidentally broke the little finger (pinky) of my hand. It was painful for a while, but after coming back home and seeing it all swelled up. I noticed a very strange, human behavior. Everything I could've done and I used to do with that finger, now wait on second, and Think about what the little finger can do? The human behavior I observed was, after getting hurt even the smallest of tasks that I used to do with that finger or even with that hand, started haunting me in a way I felt regret and bad for what I did to myself and how I am missing out on things I used to do. Like scratching myself on the side of the nose. It made me realize a few things,

Firstly, I never felt how glad I am to have this finger from which I can scratch, but when I wasn't able to do it. I felt pity for myself.

Secondly, even the smallest of things, in our surroundings provide us with meaning. But we overrule their importance because we are too consumed in this fantasy, we run after in our heads. We are all blessed to be able to contribute and bring value to existence. If only a person realizes how lucky he is to be born and fulfill the purpose of nature. We as humans are ungrateful. The first thing you my friend should start practicing is being grateful. Grateful for being alive, grateful for all the things going right in our lives. Gratitude is the best antidote of sadness, pain, and anxiety. And the repellent to your negativity, and my friend once you have control over your negativity. You will be virtually unbreakable.

Anger

Talking about control, the emotion which we all struggle with while to our own respected measures is our anger. Our frustration, exhaustion, and the thought of less authority are the reasons for anger. Remember, you can only practice your anger where you have some sort of authority or you are anonymous. So the most difficult emotions to control, in the process of Self Control can be anger. As the Blessed Prophet (saw) rightly said,

"The strongest among you is not the one, who is a greater wrestler but the one who can control himself when he is angry"

In order to stop being angry, we need to go in depth on why we get angry, we get angry when things do not go in our favor or how we plan it to be which jeopardizes the thought of things going not how we planned. to control our anger we simply need to understand one of the pillars of the philosophy our book is standing upon which is, life is uncertain, things don't and wouldn't go by our way more often than not. But what is certain, is how you deal with the uncertainty. As I said, earlier it's never the situation but how you perceive it. And most importantly,

"Anger is practiced only where the fear is less".

Become strong and learn to control before it controls you, as they say

"Never make a decision when angry, and a commitment when happy"

As Imam Al Ghazali said, there are five causes of anger, 1. Pride, 2. Vanity, 3, Mockery, 4. Blame and 5. Greed. And further, the best state is moderation, when anger is balanced under the control of the intellect. And intellect, in other words, is your consciousness.

Before I myself move onto the next chapter, by controlling your emotions I do not mean, to literally suppress your emotions. Emotion is caused by how you react to a situation, problem or event caused in our life. And how you deal with them is not by snubbing them off that would just bottle them up until they eventually burst out. Rather listen to your emotions hear them out, give them the voice of reason and the solution to the problem. Satisfy them, move one and gain peace. Most importantly, HEALING TAKES TIME, DO NOT RUSH THE PROCESS.

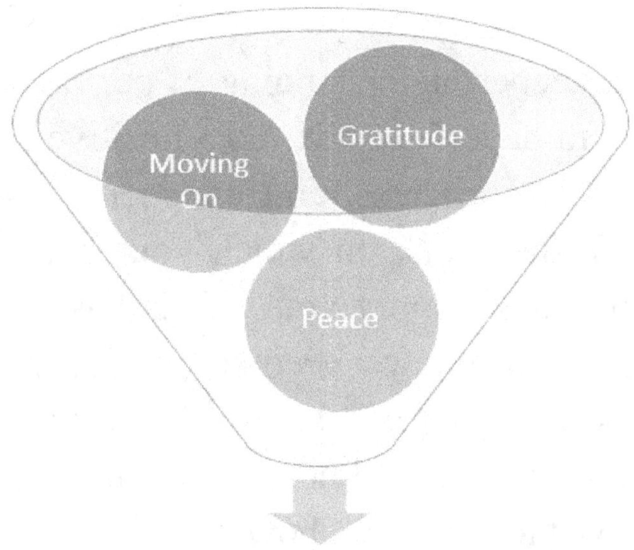

Emotional Stability

To have a further deeper perspective on emotions and self-control, I highly recommend you to not skip the next unit and the last chapter :)

Chapter # 2

GROWING THE MINDSET

ith a deeper understanding of our emotions, we need to have the right and a positive mindset in order to progress and prosper in life. The mindset is the roots, on which your belief system, perspective and simply your life is based upon. To grow the mindset, we need to go deeper into the behaviors, thoughts and approaches a person takes. In a ride to evolve and adapt, we find answers and perspectives to whys and hows.

Thoughts Becomes Things

One thing, we all forget and I am here to emphasize on that, as I did in the section earlier. Which is "control", now your mind is the president of your country, which is your life. Everything you see, do or think, is consciously or subconsciously a result of some pattern, thinking, or assumption of your mind.

You adapt to your surroundings and you become what you think. Your perception is everything. Recently I was reading a book summary of, vibration thought written in 1904 by Willam Walker. The book was on the law of attraction on simply how vibrations around and inside our brain react to how we perceive our thoughts as, and how you see and become what to perceive and dream. Like attracts like, your mind is like a magnet it attracts what you feed it. As Allah SWT says in a Hadith e Qudsi **"I bestow upon a person, what he expects from me"** Thoughts becomes things, thoughts have the vibrations that are automatically drawn parallel back to you. It's just our thoughts are uncertain, inconsistent and most importantly tempered by the society, system and fears. There would obviously be obstacles and uncertainty, but what we need is clarity of thoughts, a proper structure and patience, which can only be achieved by a rewiring the mind.

"Your life is directly proportional to the way you perceive it"

You would've heard many inspirational stories in your life about resilience and defiance. Ever wonder, how they manage to win big. It's never about talent, money, IQ, education. It's the power of your mindset. Your thoughts do not care about if you are thinking positive or not, you will get oppertunites to whatever you think. If all you think is, fear, frustration and negativity you will get opportunites to get scared, get frustrated and pity yourself and your life, it's such a simple, yet so secret law that actually works. One of the reason we get stuck in the loop of pain and misery is because that is all we think, have you ever experienced sometimes when you really don't want to get late, you get late exactly than? Our thoughts are way more and just a image, they have the power to come true. Only if you are conscious enough and have control over to think about what you want and how you want it. That's the power of your mindset.

When you want to do or be something in life, you just do it. It's as simple as that, but we doubt ourselves, we take people's comments too personally, we compare our today with someone's tomorrow and most importantly we find excuses. Your life becomes through what you feed yourself if it's positive you would see and react positively to even the worst of situations but if it's negative all you will see is negative and how you would react would be negative.

"The world as we have created it is a process of our thinking. It cannot be changed without changing our thinking."

— Albert Einstein

Life is about Balance

Everything in life would have a good impact and a negative impact with respect to your belief system, perspective, and culture. But one thing I am certain about is, in order to have a positive and impactful mindset, we definitely need to have the skill to think unbiasedly from each side. As humans, we are unable to be completely unbiased in anything, but we can surely try. Similarly, excess of everything is bad. For example, we hear "live the moment" and "work hard" all the time. If we "work hard" all the time, there wouldn't be any time to look back on, especially considering times and situations change with every second. Likewise, if we just live in the moment. There wouldn't be any moment to live for in the near future. Similarly, in everything you do.

You need to find a balance. I am someone who lives his life in the grey area in the middle, I am neither a rightist nor a leftist, and I am a centrist. And let me tell you I am at the most peace. I have access to both the parties. And I have the best view in town, to judge and see with respect to my perspective. But in life, being in the middle helps you understand the situation, whatever it may be better. And you are away from the toxicity of bias and unnecessary hate. **Nothing is harmful in life, until we fail to channel and maneuver it appropriately**.

Likewise, the life of this world or Jannah? Obviously, both. But you achieve both, by staying in the middle a bit of both, with being inclined to one side a little more than the other.

Life Is Not a Television Commercial

Life is not a 60 second television commercial through which they influence you to buy their products. Life isn't the 5 second ending with hugs and laughters. In life you would have disappointments, uncertainty, pain, hardships, and anxiety, in relationships, work, mentally and even physically. That's the reality of life and it is the pain that makes happiness so special, it is the uncertainty that makes certainty nice and it is the problems in life which truly adds a perspective to living.

The first step to a certain mindset is honesty and awareness, so this life is meant to be hard, harsh and humiliating. That's uncertain, we cannot do much about it, but what we can do is, understand our resources so efficiently, we face them purposefully and gracefully.

The Want for Validation

Ever wondered, why someone becomes a drug addict? Why do people brag about their status, appearance, and even ancestors/cast, and how people do all types of weird stuff on social media? All answers to that is approval, appreciation, and relevance. Now, it's not a bad thing, as we all have a built-in instinct of demanding validation, for some, it's just a group of people. For some, it can be as many as possible. But we all need it, we desire for it, we crave it. Why do we make fun of someone or why does anyone make fun of you? Why do people bully? Why do we tweet our hearts out? In almost everything we do publicly, there are bits if not all of the factors of validation involved. Another example of this would be, ever seen how people buy expensive brands that they themselves do not even like wearing? Validation is interrelated to satisfaction and dopamine hit. That's why when you see likes on your new Instagram post, you get satisfied and find a weird pleasure. Why does a young person become an addict? In 87% of the times it's the bad company and influence, why though? Whatever my friends do, why would it affect me? Well, it might be the case the coolest/most relevant dude in your group may be into smoking. As humans, it's our instinct we develop our habits by what we see around us. For example, your accent, did you have a choice, or did you just adapt it from your parents and friends? Similarly, when the coolest dude smokes, you are automatically super fascinated by the idea of smoking and eventually you start doing it. There's nothing wrong with asking for validation or appreciation. Do understand, there is nothing wrong with anything you do if you can manage or control it appropriately. Just we need to channel our desire and craving to the right means. In fact, it is reasonable for anyone to want their ideas, choices, achievements, or opinions validated by those around them. After all, what is the first thing we do as children when we get a good grade? We look to our parents for recognition that we did a good thing. Similarly, even after knowing that we did a good job, why does an employee look to the boss or the student to the teacher?

Likewise, Validation is part of being inter-dependent and relying on the feedback and encouragement of others around us. Even independent people still need validation in some aspects of their life, for example as I am writing this book. I would be looking at the reviews and recommendations in order to have a bigger picture. Saying that I should be able to accept my own self-validation if I do not get the response or the right feedback.

The problem arises when self-validation is not possible or is not valued. In other words, if an individual puts the opinion, approval, or recognition of someone else over their own, they will need that external, other person's validation on an ongoing basis.

The reason I started the new section, with a topic like validation is that, validation just like ego, jealousy, and comparing are built-in humanly tendencies, one cannot stop any of them but control/tailor them. If someone tells you they do not get jealous or they are not egoistic, they are virtually lying as that's not possible as long as you're alive. It's a constant battle you fight against yourself. You would see topics like comparing, validation, and ego swirling around the next few chapters in accordance with their effect and impact in that specific context.

So, the next time you tell anyone "I told you so" wait, and digest in your mind why I am saying this, and what will it do? Increase my worth, blush my ego, or just another craving of validation.

The Dopamine Detox

I talked about how validation can be a reason for someone to start smoking and how it gives us pleasure. That pleasure is produced through the chemicals in our mind that get excited over us doing something that causes self-approval. That state is called "dopamine effect". We can have a dopamine effect, on stuff as "likes" on a post to work out. It can also be known as the rewarding system in our mind, and let's be honest who doesn't appreciate rewards. It is quite interrelated with validation.

Ever wonder why we find playing video games easier than reading a book or even watching pornography rather than playing in the park? Well, all our bad habits are related to dopamine. The chemicals of pleasure, and the molecule that secretly has been controlling our lives for the longest.

In the earlier chapter, I talked about how every mood or feeling you have indirectly in relation to our minds. In this chapter, I will further diagnose with you, how with proper planning our brains we can actually gain control over our lives.

Now, dopamine like everything else in our lives isn't just bad. It in fact transmits massive, Motivation, Focus, and Interest. Dopamine can also be called a "molecule of more". As anything that releases dopamine (pleasure) in our head. You would automatically be motivated and focused to get it. And quitting that can cause the mind to feel sad and lonely.

I told you, have control over those wild cats!

And the way to control is simple, through awareness and resistance. I discussed it in the earlier few pages. Mindset is everything. Now a smart strategy could be, both eating junk food and working out give us dopamine. Here's a hack!

You know how they say, to stop the bigger evil

we choose the lesser evil. Similarly, try stopping the dopamine down while fasting through the bad ones. Have exams can't leave the gaming console? Bring some junk food, as in this modern age. Companies add as much flavor, to release as much dopamine in order for the consumer to not stop eating. So start preparing, while eating some chips, in order to keep the dopamine deficiency away.

But that being said, I myself have been a social smoker, I myself was addicted to pornography in the early half of my teenage, I have been a junk food lover for years, and so on and so forth.

I am sharing my deeper vulnerabilities with you right here, to let you know. Firstly, I don't want to keep a Messiah (the most pious) look. We all have a past, and this happens so that you learn from it. If I haven't done all of this, I probably wouldn't have been able to write this book right now. Secondly, to inspire you on how I have done some of the most common and destructive things myself, just like most of us and managed to come out of them all.

It's been 4 years since I have not consumed any inappropriate content, it's been a good three years since I stopped smoking. I haven't tried any exercises, methods or techniques. Just and only just the realization and the will.

The Infinite Cycle of Desire

I talked about happiness in detail in the last chapter, I told you why running behind happiness isn't the best of ideas. Now I will talk deep into why chasing "happiness" isn't the right idea. Why "do what makes you happy" is dumb advice. As humans, we are controlled by so many internal and external factors, many I have already talked about, a few I will talk about. The major idea of the book itself is to empower your consciousness against the idols we have created for ourselves. Happiness itself is a byproduct of desires.

A smoker smokes because it brings him "happiness", a young man masturbates in order to take pleasure as pleasure is the byproduct of happiness. A young person cheats on his very healthy marriage, why?! In order to achieve happiness and satisfy his desires. Why do people harass? Why do people blackmail? I can take these examples to extremes.

The reality is our idea of happiness is based upon the desire and pleasure of the mind. What is mood and cravings, just a call of desire to be fulfilled? All our dopamine, validation falls under this, the pursuit of desire.

Desire is a deep dark well, which has no starting or ending point. Once you try satisfying it, filling it up. It would ruin your mental, emotional, spiritual, and even physical life. But the lust would never end.

There is a reason, I believe in spirituality. There is a reason, the very base of my perspective connects with the roots of my beliefs. Why?

Because core values and beliefs protect a man, from the never-ending cycle of following your desire and lust.

"It's the integrity that helps a man fight desires"

It's the integrity that sets the bottom line for a person, it's the integrity that helps the person think bigger. And it's the integrity to which a person should follow in order to find peace.

In this noisy and materialistic world, it's the honor and integrity of a person, that helps them stand apart, focused, and in peace.

"The constant chasing of desires makes a person vacant from the inside"

Desire is an enemy bigger than any other, and to fight, is hard. But in fighting lies a person's true purpose. A purpose, that doesn't make him happy or rich. But that benefits him and the betterment of humanity. This is where the power of intention comes in, your intention is your biggest strength, motivation and edge. Your intention is your purpose, your purpose is what keeps you focused and yout focus should always benefit the community in one way or another.

"And my friend, you cannot change the world, if the only thing you see is your desire and pleasure"

With the help of some realization from the Almighty, I found the will and grit. To initiate fight against my inner evil, and this right here can be a potential awakening for you as well. This can be your gift of realization if you are ready to take it. Or you can stay in the cell of your ego, run after pleasure and complain about how peaceful life is. (A deeper perception continued in the last chapter)

Ego is Enemy

Ryan Holiday, thank you for the heading. Anyhow, the ego can be the biggest enemy of a person. A person's ego affects everything from spiritual life to its relationships, financial life, and most importantly mental health. If you are a part of your mind, trying to somehow justify ego, with some Instagram quote you read a few days ago, that's ego hiding ego itself. **"The bigger the man's head becomes, the easier it gets to fill in his shoes"**

One of the worst things an ego does, is to mentally surround yourself in a delusional box of self-appraisal very apart from actuality. It starts where our notion of ourselves and the world grows so strong that it begins to distort the reality which surrounds us.

In your head, you become so much "superior" and better, you start to look down upon people, relationships, and even practices. In a keyboard battlefield, how often do we have the courage to let the other person actually "win" the argument or accept that your opinion was authentic? How often do we see long proven friendships gone in the way of ego? On something as small as "apologizing" I know we all know all this stuff, but if we all know it. Why don't we work on it?

So I was having a discussion with my best friend

about ego, the other day and she said something which was quite interesting and made sense to me. She was like, you would always see the wealthier man with more ego than the poorer. I would put her point across, we all know arrogance is the byproduct of ego. But **"we are only able to practice ego where we can, rather on whom we can "** and it's the one privileged who can practice it.

Now Ego isn't just being superior or better, ego is the desire of mind and the soul to be heard, to stand-out and to posses the authority, I talked earlier about how the one privileged can practice it, by privilege I do not only mean, financially or physically but anything from excuses, pain, challenges can also be considered as privileged. . Being privileged of a bad memory to which we can further share to express how our life is more fu*ked than others, to somehow justify our excuses. How often we compare our challenges or our pains with others, trying to portray how damn difficult our life is, and how nobody can understand. It is one of the ways how our mind feels esteemed and stand-out

Ego is the hunger of validation and esteem in your mind, ever heard or observed how we often say, I might be the worst but I don't lie or how we say I never lie! We consider it as "awareness" but it's the ego. Because in life nothing is constant, it's not like because I control my ego, I am not egoistic. It's a consistent battle that would not stop up until your dead and till than you have to fight it, regularly and every single time.

The difference between Self Esteem and Ego

Ego as I said earlier, pushes the self into these delusional walls, apart from the actuality. Isolated in a room of "being always right". It's not like anyone wants to be egoistic, it's just they confuse their ego over themselves. With all honesty, I have been in that state of the mind for a while myself. It's a dark place, and it leaves you alone. In which you cannot differ or feel anything wrong by yourself but everyone around you starts to distance themselves from you and you get lost in your mind on how can I be egoistic? "I am just defending myself, you know as they say never let anyone else dictate you. How can I be egoistic? Oh it might be a misunderstanding and they just cannot understand me" (the voice inside the head)

Self-esteem, on the other hand, is your right to the basic principles, laws, and choices in social and cultural norms and values respectfully.

Here are a few habits you can do to evolve your mindset and tame your ego. **Learn to appreciate**, always **keep a smile** on your face, defeat the ego with facts and always remember how you were born.

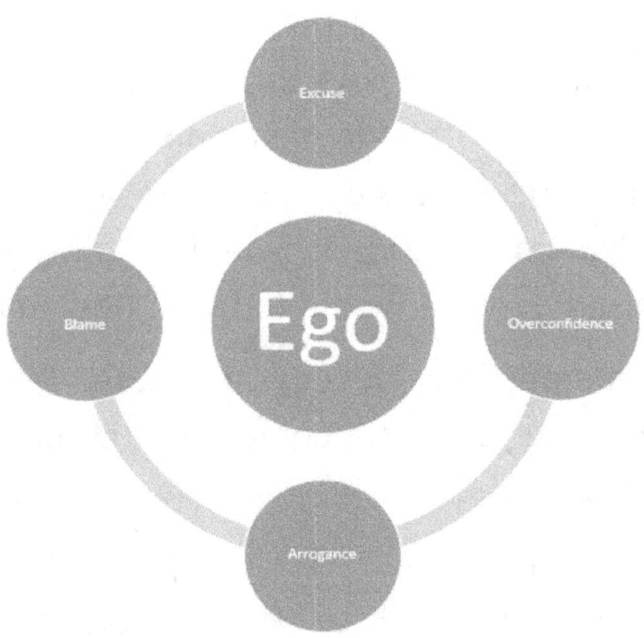

The illusionary bubble of ego protected by its guards

Comparison is Cruel

Comparing is something we all do whether it maybe heights, phones, or even decisions. Comparing is a human phenomenon, we compare everything, from health to wealth. In fact, how often we see whenever we fail an exam or make a blunder, the first thing we do to calm our parents and elders is tell them that we were not alone and how that awesome son of your friend also failed. Similarly, whenever we are down and feeling bad, one of the things we tell ourselves is that we are not alone, and everyone goes through hard times and all. Similarly, how often do we compare people, brands, and places because they are at par with each other? With that being said, I wouldn't tell you to stop comparing, rather I would tell you, how to compare.

Rule number #1. Never compare the final product or results, for example comparing the net worth, or followers, or even the way of living.

Rule Number #2. To compare yourself with someone, you need to know from where they started, how many hours per week they invested and the struggles they faced.

Rule Number #3. Never compare yourself to someone with your own shoes.

Rule Number #4. While doing all that, don't forget to have a long and deep look into the emotions of the other person.

Here you go my friends, these are the rules to comparison. Now compare all you want. As you will have to do years of research on the other person before you collect any data and analyze it. Jokes aside, it's really easy for us to assume something while looking at someone's today and comparing our self with them. It's virtually impossible to compare someone while being true to every aspect of one's life.

That being said, you have no alternative. You are who you are, and you stay who you are. There is no point in comparing when you have no choice or alternative to replace yourself with any. You are a human being, not a handbag.

"It's the circumstances, that make a person unique and the past that helps them grow"

Human Potential

The true potential of a human being is a mystery that no test, no device or no brain itself can solve. Human brain is such a complex yet powerfully wired, no one truly knows what a person is capable except the creator himself.

All the internal and external calamities and uncertainty we face, whether it be insecurity, illness or even misfortune. Think about all these calamities as the speed breakers on your highway, but your road is capable to be driven fast, that is why it needed speed breakers. Some roads have more speed breakers then other according to the capacity of the road or a huge contract or a lousy engineer (which is not applicable as per we are concerned).

Let's dive in a little deep to this, your vehicle which is your life, on the road which is your journey is filled with speed breakers and stops. Which road needs speed breakers? The one which has the potential to be driven fast upon. Speed breakers might slow us, but they shouldn't be able to stop us.

That being said, we live in a society where we make fishes climb trees and make monkey's swim. And then we talk about how we are not as good as someone or how we are not talented and even how below far we are.

Successful and unsuccessful people do not vary greatly in their abilities. They vary in their desires to reach their potential." – John Maxwell

There is nothing that limits the human mind except death. There is no limit to a human brain, just stop racing, competing and comparing potentials with one another, as that's truly a baseline of human brain, being judged and compared by someone or something with someone or something completely different. For example, horses with birds. Everyone is born different, with different purposes. Such cliché yet impossible to truly implement. **Comparison is not just the thief of joy, but the constant cycle of grief, disappointments and dissatisfaction.**

There is no such thing as "impossible" for a human mind, just the monkey would need years of hard work in order to compete with a baby fish in swimming. The fish is born with an advantage just like the monkey is born with an advantage. A fish no matter how resilient or skillful it may be, just cannot survive on the surface. That does not mean the monkey is better than the fish or the fish is dumb or how we say in our desi terminology "nalayaq" just born to carter different problems, structured to survive different environment and simply born with a different purpose.

"Never become a byproduct of someone's opinion"

The Rat Race

Very similar, to comparison, we do another thing in life which disturbs our peace of mind the most is, we compete. We are programmed from a very young age to compete and to always be at the top and everything of that sort. It doesn't kill someone, to be in the first position. However, your competition isn't with anyone else but yourself.

So recently, I was reading this article on a book written by Simon Sinek, where he talks about his visit to the education summit of two leading tech companies, Apple and Microsoft. What he saw was very interesting about the approach and the mindset of both the companies, the 70% of the Microsoft presentations were on how they can defeat Apple, and whereas there wasn't a single presentation from Apple about Microsoft or any other "competitors" in fact they were consumed on how they can solve more problems.

You see a pattern here? Microsoft had a finite vision, dependent on Apple's growth. Whereas, Apple becoming such a huge empire focuses on the problems ahead, which are almost infinite.

Now if you apply this at a micro level, we come

to see there is no competition with anyone but yourself. Similarly, if an athlete competes in their mind with the other one, their performance would be limited to how the other player performs. For example, a footballer scored 30 goals in a season, someone who would be competing with him, would have a target of 30 to chase. Which can potentially hurt his chances of scoring 50 odd goals that season.

Competing can very easily divert a person from the purpose to egotistically trying to get the better of the other person.

The healthy competition, in reality, is to complete with your previous self and grow every single day ahead.

The Dungeon of Incorrect Thinking

Overthinking a word we hear a lot, something we all do and something perceived as evil and as destructive as anything. Although Overthinking just likes, the comparison is something we all do and we do it nonstop. As our conscious brain is born to think, analyze, and find out solutions. It will think, it always thinks tirelessly as long as your organs of the brain are alive. The brain is like a kid in a superstore, it will look for something to play with. It could be wise of you to help him play with something less disturbing. But too much of pampering can make it crave for more and too much ignoring can make it rebellious.

"Avoid being excessively suspicious, for some suspicion is a sin" (49-12)

The desire of your brain to fulfill its job of "thinking" should never be satisfied by thinking about the possibility of your own future or past. Ever noticed how we always have a solution for other's problems, but never for our own? You know why that happens because with our problems there are emotions attached whereas, with someone else's problems, we are not emotionally connected. Remember how I said, never let your emotions blind you? This is what I meant by that.

Anyhow, why you shouldn't think about your past or future and all the possibilities of what might happen and what could've happened, this is a kind of thinking that wastes your time and energy and prevents you from acting, doing new things, and making progress in your life.

One of the most destructive things that happen

due to incorrect thinking is, not only do you get stuck in a loop of assumption and pity but also it deviates the mind from its true purpose which is, to find solutions to the problems rather than getting stuck in them.

As in life, the problems would never stop, once you solve your problem it would automatically be replaced by another one. The problem-free, happy life we are advertised, only exists in heaven. Similarly, with problems, we feel insecure, and with insecurity, we feel worse for our problems.

The easiest way I learned from Mark Manson's book was, the only way you stop overthinking about your problems and you focus on solving them, by accepting your problems and working on solving them.

It's like telling yourself, I might not be in a good state at the moment but if I am not in a better place, in a month's or weeks' time, it's my fault. Regardless of what happened and how it happened, that's uncertainty, you cannot control that but what you can control is, how you further deal with it. For example, your loved one got hurt in a car accident. That's uncertain and unforeseen but how you react to it is the art of dealing with the problem, rather than blaming it on the nature, car driver or your luck, because once you get diverted from the task of solving the problem, to thinking about it and its various possibilities. It's not the easiest of habits to come out of.

Again, thinking is an act you cannot stop, it's a part of your body that works and is created to work, constantly till the heart fails and the blood stops passing. There is no such thing as "overthinking" it's just right thinking and wrong thinking. As mentioned before, constantly thinking about the past or the future and all the possibilities is the wrong way of thinking, as it provides you with no value but costs you highly. Whereas, a scientist or an economist thinking hard and long on a new scientific problem to solve or how to get the country out of an economic crisis is definitely the "right" thinking regardless of how much time you spent.

The word "over" in this context represents "excess" whereas, as shown in the example earlier excess of right and purposeful thinking isn't bad but the excess of wrong and pointless thinking is. As you cannot do anything about your past and are unaware of the future is in actuality what's destructive.

Learn to Say "No"

Saying "no" is the actual thing that would set you apart in life. Saying no, actually helped me grow in life in more than one way.

"A man is known by the company he keeps as well as you are a sum of five friends you have"

Back in my early teens, I had a very typical company. With all respect to them, they had this toxic static life pattern and mindset. I remember talking to one of them a few months back. And from the last four years or so, my whole life took a 360-degree twist. And they are still stuck in the same mindset.

Anyhow, all we used to do was, smoke in the car talk about girls, blush each other's ego and that's it. And in and day out, the same thing over and over and over again for months.

Just one day, I realized what am I doing with myself and why am I doing it? But I was too afraid of being rejected by them and making them disappointed, I carried on.

Up until I come to a point in my life, I just totally started ignoring them. Ignoring their calls, ignoring their messages. And with all honesty, that short term disappointment helped me a long way.

Another way, saying "no" helped me, was the mindset. Whenever people used to bully me, whenever teachers used to underestimate me, whenever the voice inside my own head used to doubt me. One thing, I used to tell myself was "NO" PERIOD.

NO, I AM **NOT** A LOSER, **NO**, I AM **NOT** A QUITTING, **NO**, I AM **NOT** DUMB. **NO**, I WILL **NOT** FEEL PITY FOR MYSELF. **NO**, I DON'T CARE. **NO**, I CAN DO IT.

Likewise, life is about choice. You cannot do everything and be with everyone and stay healthy at the same time. Why? Because in life we have very scarce time.

With every action, we do, whether it is self-pity or reading a book. We are trading it with some other thing we could've done at the same time. Never let someone else, make your choices in life. Whether it is staying depressed over being happy or wasting your time in regret rather than living it. And if we are not able to say "no" to our bad company, say "no" to our regret, anxiety and even past. Say "no" to our doubter and **say no, to find the ultimate YES! In our lives.**

Finding the Direction

Almost all of us struggle or have struggled with questions like what is our purpose, how to find our passion, how to be successful, what is our talent, and how to find it. These are some of the questions we all face.

"Who determines (the capacities and faculties) and furnishes them with (appropriate) guidance to achieve the final goal" (83:7)

Passion is overrated

How often you see people, starting something very passionately and ending due to burnout. The reality is, passion is a selfish approach. As it demands on what my job or my side hustle can give me. For a very long while and sometimes not as long, we run after the satisfaction and pleasure we get by doing that, so and so thing. But to keep the passion running we either would have to achieve highly and consistently or we have to get motivated by the financial factors.

We often hear, in fact, we hear all the time. Do

what you love, do what makes you happy, etc. That's never a lasting approach, to be very honest knowing the human behaviors. We just cannot get satisfied by doing the same thing again and again, until we change our mindset from "getting" to "giving".

Rather than passion, we should have the craftsman mindset and think about how we can value the world, through your product, entertainment, or information. With this mindset, your focus becomes to improve your skill and provide better service rather than getting pleasure out of it.

And this it can be your purpose. Your purpose in specific life is to provide value to the world with your product and contribute to the welfare of nature and become a mean of the Almighty, to help someone with something through your ultimate skill, which itself is blessed within you for a reason.

With saying all this, there are four major aspects in finding your purpose and profession for life. Here is the most frequent advice anyone gives you when you ask them for what profession you should choose. The most famous answer is, do something which has "scope" in the market. Then there is the motivational speaker theory of doing what you love and do what your heart tells you, very less but there are some people who tell you do something for the society and lastly, do something you are good at.

The reality of the matter is, to find the profession from which you wouldn't burnout or need breaks and even retirement is when you find something which fulfills all of the above factors. Passion, Income, Value to the society, and something you are genuinely good at. This four aspect equation is also known as Ikigai, the Japanese secret to a long and happy life.

The circle Of Ikigai that would help you find your purpose, that would give you income, something you are skilled at, something the world needs and something you love doing and are passionate about.

Stop chasing "passion" it's not durable.

Talent is a Deceiving

Talent is one of the most overrated phenomena in our society and in our minds. Which ultimately becomes as big of an excuse for us not doing well in our lives. I read this book named Grit by Angela Duckworth. In which she talks about how talent isn't really required at every stage. For example, for me to become the best cricketer of my neighborhood, I do not need an extreme amount of talent or any talent at all. But hard work and skill.

As "Hard Work beats talent, when talent doesn't work hard enough" (not mine)

Similarly to be a freelancer or to a good dancer at a party. You do not need talent but effort, passion, and skills. Talent is important, but talent is the extraordinary form of skill and command. You only truly need when competing with extraordinary people of your specific field. For example, learning guitar isn't a talent but a skill. But doing amazing things with it can be a talent.

How often we see talent failing but the resilience and hard work succeeding. I can't stop myself from giving another cricketing example, Umar Akmal was a young, classy Pakistani batsman. Who took the world by storm with his brilliant timing and wrist work. But all he had was Talent. He failed miserably after making a fine impact. Now he has the same amount of test centuries as Yasir Shah (a tailender)

So the key to success isn't always being talented but being resilient, patient, resourceful, and work.

Talking about Success.

Success is such a big mystery, we all are running behind. When we hear the word, "successful" we have a dude coming out from a yellow Lamborghini in his Armani suit. Most often than not, we judge "successfulness" with numbers. Whether it is followers or bank balance.

All our lives, we have been taught if you do not study well, you wouldn't get a job. If you don't get a job, you wouldn't have a great lifestyle and if you don't have a great lifestyle you would be "unsuccessful".

Success can be anything for anyone, a success for

a housewife can be cooking a delicious meal, a success for a singer might be selling 10k albums, and for an entrepreneur to make 100k sales. Success can be from getting a star on your homework to I don't know maybe writing a book.

As per 2017 Billal's words,

"Success is something you feel, rather than something you earn"

Structuralism

"Goals are for losers" (Scott Adams)

In order to achieve anything in life whether, that be a goal or a mindset. You need proper structure and long term planning. In order to achieve your goals, you need to stop focusing on them. Rather restructure your daily routine, into small sets of work you do consistency, in order to eventually reach whatever your goal might be. As the thought of achieving your respective goal can be a fascinating picture to imagine. But in order to lose weight, earn money, or gain subscribers. You need a proper structure of long term strategy and consistent effort.

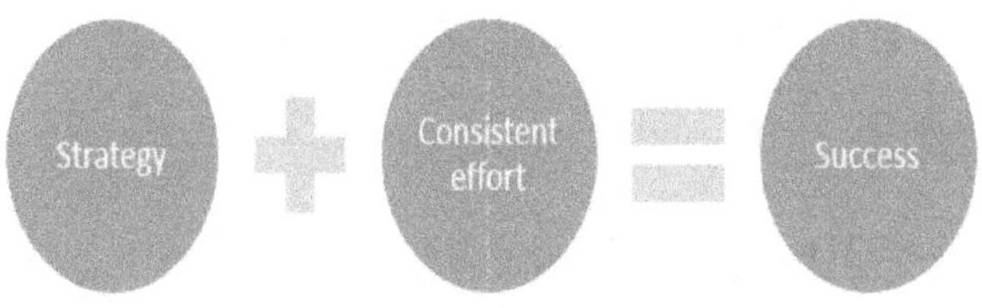

How often do we see people quitting their goal of losing weight, after checking the weighing machine every day, as they see no difference at all?

Similarly, everyone has goals and dreams, but not everyone is ready to work on them through short but consistent effort. That's why we don't see too many goals being achieved. Further why? Because we are too ambitious, impatient and we crave for instant gratification way too much.

Want to build a brand, become an artist, or quit smoking? This is the real path to you achieving your respective goals. List down on a paper, your goal, why you want to achieve it, and how you can contribute every day to your cause. And once it's done, forget about the goal and focus on structure/system. In order to move forward in life and further be in the best possible position in achieving the goals. As you only achieve your goals, when you stop focusing on them and start working on them with a proper structure and consistent effort, if you improve just 1% a week, you will be 52% better than previous year.

Why stop focusing on the goals? Excess of visualizing and thinking about your goals, can put you in a state of fantasy and pleasure, after which stopping to think can become really hard, and when you visualize yourself achieving your goals and wake up to the reality and find out you have done nothing and there is so much yet to be done.

We find it easier to quit.

The Excuse Loophole

Talent, as well as improper comparison and jealousy, can make a person trapped in the vicious denial phase, in which you have a counter-argument to stop yourself from not performing well. Also, an "excuse" to not appreciate someone who did well, in whatever way or thing possible.

Not only do we look for stuff to hide our shortcomings, we neglect to appreciate the other person's achievements. Which is one of the most destructive things to have for as mindset as it is a sign of high ego? (This is one of the examples of excuse and a very common one)

But the excuse mindset does something which is even worse than ego. It snubs the whole base of growth, which is Accepting, Learning, and Working Smarter. It rejects the idea of admitting the failure or admitting your mistake. This puts a person in such a negative thought process for everything and anything, we would have an excuse, from which would be able to deceive people and hide our shortcomings. But in reality just our immaturity and negligence.

Now excuse is something we all make, whether it is on how you came late to the class to why couldn't you submit the project on time.

"There's an excuse in every reason and a reason in every excuse"

There is a very little fine line between reason and excuse, for example in my 9th grade. I genuinely used to get sick a lot. But most of the time, more than a reason it was an excuse. Do realize, there will always be a dot from which you create a circle and a drop from which you create a lake.

But never surround yourself into the dark loop of excuses, you would not only neglect growth. You would also feed our ego. For example, I can make great videos. Just I do not have the right equipment. You didn't just make an excuse, but you also satisfied your ego. By now only giving an excuse but also demolishing someone else's hard work under the advantage of equipment. Learn to accept, appreciate and evolve.

And in reality, life is about defying limits and being resourceful on what you have. Because in life there is no such thing as a perfect circumstance. You just have to adapt and overcome.

"Our greatest weakness lies in giving up. The most certain way to succeed is always to try just one more time." – Thomas A. Edison

A Life with Zero Shits

The world has been partial, free from slavery.

But are we really?

"Mainstream system is the slavery of the twenty-first century"

One of the most common questions a person faces in life is what is my Ikigai, what is something I am good at. And it's not a question we ask ourselves for a certain time. But it's a lifetime question. But think about it, are you doing what you are great at? And if you are, what alternative have you ever tried or experienced to come to this conclusion?

The reality is, due to the peer pressure and the system created in our society, we are almost obligated to follow it. Whether it may be 16 years of investment in"education" or anything else in life from dressing to marriage. We are manufactured under the system of extreme ordinary.

I asked my banker friend this question, are you "great" at what you do? He was like, well, kind of. I am expecting a promotion, and I haven't been fired yet. I think I am good enough at my job. I was like, okay so you think you are meant for this job? He replied, yes I think, as I am not interested in being lawyers, I didn't have the grades for pursuing medical education, so yeah. I feel banking was the option for me.

That made me realize that we live such a scripted life and whenever we want to experiment in our lives. We have peer pressure, hurdles which drive us away from our designated purpose. And limit us to the mainstream fields and the blind following of the market. But why do we limit ourselves? It's the fear of being indifferent and judged. A fear that can easily deviate anyone from their purpose, peace and even originality. **"We live a scripted life not that we need to but we have too"** we live a scripted life, in order to work in the society, we have to live a scripted life to be accepted in the society. I am going through the conventional system of education, not that I need to but I have to for the peace of mind of my loved ones, very frankly all the things I have in my portfolio at the moment are the things I have done without following the mainstream system, from starting a podcast to writing this book and becoming a life coach. The reality is the scripted life we all have to follow, "way more than religiously" does nothing but limits a human brain and potential to nothing but alphabets, numbers and symbols.

Numbers will always be scars, that's the harsh reality of life, Number can never be enough, you will always have "lesser grades, income, strength and even vision than someone else, likewise you would always have something more than someone else.

"Not everything that can be counted counts and not everything that counts can be counted" (Albert Einstein)

One of the major reasons why I see most of the people are me, sad, dissatisfied, lonely and anxious is, because they all are running behind something, wether it be the first position or the bank balance even followers in our day and age. Not knowing their purpose, existence and even themselves, why? Because they never had the courage to step out of their zone, defy their negativity and gain control.

Message of Hope

I have talked about, success, goals, mindset and how they all affected and matter in a certain mindset, but what truly motivates the self, heals the wounds and empower growth is Hope. Hope is the thought which is direcetly inclined to change and growth. All these positivity, control and stability comes after the vison of hope, never lose hope. Hope is the essence of life. Many of us could not even live a life of peace without having hope deep inside the heart. Life is unpredictable, hard and quite notorious at times. Things go out of hand and beyond of our control many times. Hope helps us keep the fight on and improves the chances of making our life better. **The Certainty mindset is powered by the hope, hope is further powered by ambition and ambition attracts the law of**

attraction.

"Never let anyone take away your superpower of hope"

IT IS THE INTELLCT OF A PERSON WITH THE KNOWLEDGE OF THE SELF THAT SAVES THE MAN FROM ENDLESS DESIRES, COMPARISONS AND DISSATISFACTION. CERTAINTY STARTS WITH AWARENESS OF THE NEGATIVITY AND ENDS WITH THE HUNGER OF PEACE AND PURPOSE WITH HOPE BEING THE WAY AND POSITIVITY THE ROAD.

The best thing about life and why we can be the certain in uncertain is, no matter how uncertain the times maybe, it would always be as certain as our resistance.

CHAPTER #3

EIGHT TRANSFORMATIONAL HABITS

ere are some of the most powerful habits that Hwill not only transform your mindset but give you a positive edge in every situation and aspect of life. Whether it is emotional, practical, or spiritual. And will definitely help you in seeing life through a more energetic and positive way.

The Gratitude Hour

The hour of gratitude is a technique, I discovered back when I was all depressed in my mid teenage years. This is a technique in which you, at minimum of 15 minutes a day. Just write all the positive things you're glad for in your life. From having the necessities to may be parents or best friends. To further oxygen and the brain. It would be hard at first, you would get stuck but keep pushing yourself to think about more and more blessings and things you are grateful for in life. There would eventually come a time, in which you start finding one new thing every day.

Why practice the weekly hour of gratitude? It will psychologically put your mind in such a positive curiosity, that you will start looking at things in a positive manner to fill in the blanks every day. Which would further help you, fight your negativity as well as give your mind and perspective a greater look and peace. When you realize nothing you're not ahead or behind, you're not deprived and most importantly you are where you meant to be. And you are blessed to be able to contribute to the existence and living, trees exhale so you can inhale, ozone covers to protect you, surface stands to give you the way. You are not alone, you can never be alone.

It further continues with how many people you can make smile per hour, how you affect someone's well-being, how many people you listened too and how helpful you were to your family.

The Hydration Advantage

Intake of water is a necessity for the mind, body, and growth of all aspects. Water is the key element in the physical or mental growth of almost all living beings, whether it may be a plant or a human being.

Water is vital to life and it is often overlooked as a stress reliever. Every cell and every system in the body is dependent on water for healthy functioning. Normal daily activity causes the loss of about 2 liters (6-8 cups) of water, which must be replaced throughout the day. Our brains are composed of approximately 70% water and our blood is more than 85% water and according to research, a 5% drop in body fluids will cause a 25% to 30% loss of energy in the average person and a 15% drop in body fluids causes' death.

Some of the benefits of drinking more than 11 glasses of water a day are, less anxiety, a control in a panic attack, increase in focus and productivity, growth of muscles, growth of the mind, reduce headache, keeps the kidneys healthy, cleanse the body toxins, hydrates the skin and most importantly prevent the possibility of cancer of major kind.

In short a habit as small as drinking can be as big of a change in your mindset and life.

"Thousands have lived without love, not one without water." W. H. Auden

Early morning Enigma

We all have heard and know how waking up early is a great habit and all. But I will tell you right here step by step on how to truly make the most of this habit and why it will transform your life for good. Now firstly, something to which we wake up is one of the most essential part of how our day might be functioned. For example, waking up with a buzzer and triggering an alarm or through someone's shout isn't the healthiest way to wake up. As your brain would subconsciously be alerted and disturbed. Rather than being peaceful and active. So the first thing to do is, change the alarm sound to something, which might be loud, well because I myself cannot wake up to low and minimal sound. But it should be a sound that brings you peace and calmness. You do not want your mind to wake you up in haste and disturbance but rather in peace and calmness, as a great starting leads to a great day. Likewise, gain control of your routine rather than the deadlines controlling you.

Secondly, never open your smartphone or check your notifications right away, in fact have a warm glass of water. Take a few deep breaths, consume the toilet if you may. Freshen up, have a glass of milk or some fruits, till you open you check your updates.

I haven't read the 5am club yet, but I do know about the 20/20/20 formula and I will let you know how I apply it to my morning routine. 60 minutes = 20+20+20 minutes.

So, the first set of twenty minutes, I perform ablution (wazu), I pray Fajar and make long sweet talks through supplication and do dhrik.

The next twenty minutes, I usually go for some cycling, a bit of home work out and boxing. And in the last twenty minutes, I recite the Quran or read a soft book (as in not too consuming for the mind)

Through prayers I find peace and positivity, through workout I warm up my body and energize myself and through soft reading I activate my brain.

So, how to conquer the mornings?

Change the Alarm

Avoid checking notifications 3. Apply the 20*3 rule

Rehearsing the Pain

We all get stuck in some moments in life, mostly the "bad memories". We regret while thinking about it, it makes us sad and depressed. Whether it be bullying or a breakup. They are memories that put us in uncomfortable situations. This is a method I have used myself and I tell quite a few who text me and all. The thing is, although we think about those events and memories a lot, but we are never able to walk through them entirely, as we stop in between. The simple exercise rather than habit is, whenever the horror of fears irritate your mind in pursuit of making you sad or depressed. Rather than hiding from it, distracting yourself from it or even ignoring it to whatever extent you are able too. Just face them, and go through it. Cross question your fear to the last possible extent, "then what?", "So what?" "That's it"? Is this what I was afraid of? This exercise will not only help you move on but help you face your ultimate fears. We are scared of some moments, they are in our heads but we are never able to visualize them, go through them. Realize, even the worst and the best scenarios are bestowed with the Will of Allah, and it is the fear of Allah which kills all the other fears. Nothing can go as "wrong" as how they went with Imam Hussain (a), yet without fears. Our Imam was martyred in prostration. This itself, says a lot. "Your fear is nothing but an illusion of the mind" that scares you, so that you would not be able to move on from it.

Internal support system

This is an instinct, we should all develop. In life there would come times, more often than not when no one would believe you, your idea or even your opinion. When people would reject you, when people would ignore you for nothing. At that time, the most important thing a person needs is the voice of inside and the voice of reasons. A voice that tells her, she is the star of her own life. The story revolves around you, rather than you revolving around the story. When someone rejects you or makes wrong assumptions about you. Firstly, look inside yourself deep thoroughly and honestly. Understand and realize what went wrong, there would always be something wrong. Improve it, learn from it. After doing that develop the instinct and courage inside yourself to stick to your guns and constantly inspire yourself. Tell yourself, YOU ARE GOOD ENOUGH, YOU CAN DO IT. Remember, no matter how hard the storms might be, Allah is with you and Allah is not unfair. Care for yourself like you do for someone you are responsible for.

"So remember me, and I will remember you" (2-152)

Keeping a Smile

"Smile is the jewelry of the courageous"

Smiling is such a small yet powerful act one can definitely replicate in their lives. There would come times in your life, when you would have to fake a smile. A smile is no other than a therapy, which costs you nothing. Put it automatically, brings positive vibes into the body and outside the environment. Next time you are feeling down, try putting on a smile. There's a good chance your mood will change for the better. Smiling can trick the body into helping you elevate your mood because the physical act of smiling actually activates neural messaging in your brain.

A simple smile can trigger the release of neural communication boosting neuropeptides as well as mood-boosting neurotransmitters like dopamine and serotonin. Think of smiling like a natural antidepressant. Studies have shown that smiling releases endorphins, natural painkillers, and serotonin. Together these three neurotransmitters make us feel good from head to toe. Not only do these natural chemicals elevate your mood, but they also relax your body and reduce physical pain. Smiling is a natural drug. It boosts the immune system, lower the blood pressure and is quite contagious, as the famous aphorism goes, **"one smile can lead to the whole village smiling"**

I wonder why we don't emphasize on smiling as much as we should, but it was a definite game changer for me, in every aspect of life from mental, physical and with human interactions.

Stay a Student

The title speaks for itself, According to the definition on dictionary.com, a student is "any person who studies, investigates, or examines thoughtfully". Always have curiosity and will to learn new things and new ideas. Stay humble, respectful and curious, just like a true student. Never come to a point in life, when you start to think you know, "enough". As the difference between wisdom and arrogance is the knowledge, and how it is used by the intellect.

"Knowledge is the passport to the future, for tomorrow belongs to those who prepare for it today." Malcolm X

Healthy Sleep

A healthy sleep is as important as waking up early, if not more. As without a healthy sleep, you are unable to have a healthy morning. Just like waking up early, sleep is a whole subject, researched and studied by doctors, psychologists, athletes and even engineers. A habit, a practice and most importantly a need. Just like the 5 am club, there is a whole 600+ page book on sleep and just like 5 am club, I haven't read it yet. For anyone interested, it's called **"why we sleep"**.

Ever wonder why often wake up from a nap grumpy or have mind swings? Or what are some of the mental effects and physical effects of sleep to our life?

Here are some of the benefits of sleep, Increases

immunity, reduces stress, increase concentration, brings peace to the soul, reduces the chances of heart stroke and disabilities, helps build the muscles, refreshes the eyes, decreases anxiety, etc.

But just like everything in life, sleep is beneficial but the balance of it as well as the good healthy sleeps. Sleep more than the hours, depends on quality. One should not sleep more than twice a day, as excess of naps can seriously cause stress and anxiety.

How I sleep is, twice in the whole 24 hour time period, 5-6 hours at night and 3-4 hours at afternoon or pre dinner. Everyone has to adapt to their own routines but never compromise on our sleep especially if you at my or near about age.

"The best bridge between despair and hope is a good night's sleep.

"The goodnights sleep is the icing on your cake of productivity, efficiency and joy"

UNIT #2
SOCIAL MEDIA

CHAPTER #1

YOU

---

ocial Media, the innovation of the post 90's Ssomething, the millennials created and completely revolutionized the world, into a global illusion. I will try not to hit you with a lot of facts and figures, you not reading an article but we on a journey. And neither would I completely reject the positives of Social media, be completely frank with you, now that you are reading this book right now, there is a high possibility of 8 in 10 that you found me and this book using one of the social media platforms itself. It wouldn't be wrong in saying, I am a product of social media myself, and the opportunity social media provides is massive. But the cost you have to pay can be brutal as well. As someone who has been on social media for the longest myself and the observer I am. It's delusional, addictive, and extremely possessive. We as being the first generation of social media users are still in work at finding out the effects and affects of Social Media.

We have seen massive industrial outbreaks, we have seen social media changing the lives of individuals and firms. It's never the existence of something that bothers, but how you adapt it.

In this rather small unit, we would be discussing the ways how social media possess us and how we can defuse its harmful effects. "A harmless enemy is nothing more than a lazy friend" becomes selfish and cunning to how you use social media. Social media is a nuke for the brain if used improperly and in pursuit of certainty, we definitely need to carter this very unorthodox form of desire, lust and insecurity. As this innovation is way more lethal than any other if not used properly. We have seen people livestream genocides, we have seen disturbing cases of cyberbullying, we have seen people take their lives just because they felt uglier and smaller with comparison to that and celebrity.

Ever wondered why it has become a hobby of ours just to open a social media site, and just scroll down and down until eventually we are stopped. It's called the infinity loop or the infinity pool. Social media works on the "Attention Economy". This is simply defined as the more attention you are able to consume of the consumer the more bucks you are able to make. One of the strategies social media sites use is machine learning. Ever wondered how you are thinking about something and all of a sudden you see your feed filled with ads and posts related to that thing? I wouldn't go deep into the factual details of social media, as I may go irrelevant. But I do know one thing, handling social media is no joke. In the evolutionary invention, we have seen a whole new area of study, research, and development, we have seen the voice of layman been heard, we have the vast career opportunities but we also have seen issues such as social media anxiety, the fear of missing out aka FOMO and a rapid increase in insecurities. There is a saying in business **"You either buy the product or you are one"**

But I am not here to tell you to quit social media, rather we are here to talk about how to be two times ahead of technology and use it to our own benefit. As the algorithms, the colors and the way these applications are designed are very cruel. And the only thing they focus upon is, your attention, careless of the consequences. Understand, this is a business not a welfare project. They do not care about you as long as you see their ads and give them revenue.

Hate and Cyberbullying

We all struggle with online hate some more than others. But why do people hate on the internet, there are multiple reasons. One of which is, we all show our best versions on the internet. The perfect, glamorous, after filtered self. And it's something we all do, why well to be in accordance, relevance, and relatable to the trend and the community.

Now for someone like me, seeing someone so "perfect" I subconsciously compare them with my looks, my achievements, and most importantly the number of followers. I start to feel jealous, small, and pity for myself. To this extent I start to put in my time and effort. To try to expose and make the other person look bad to feel some sort of satisfaction and peace.

You being the typical "Allahamdulilah bought new Mercedes" or "Allahamdulilah got 20 A*" dude, just trying to enjoy your moment not realizing, you directly rubbing it on the face of someone to this extent, they do not hesitate to send hate to you publicly.

Now, please don't start with your "overly

motivated" quotes such as "haters are motivators" haters are not motivators. Like, why do you want to be motivated by someone's misery? They are your brothers, who are desperate for validation.

Now if we don't write mean comments or we resist doing that why do we have our set of reservations with a set of people on the internet. Let's be honest here. We get jealous too, we get insecure too, we dislike some people because well they might be against our values or they are just better than us in something, or simply because unlike us they are appreciated and praised. Do we feel any good about them in our heads? Or if we are candid and honest with someone, do we "appreciate" that so and so person? The reality is we all are haters to an extent, some of us might be less than the others but we all get jealous. We just hide and portray this one very cool and mature person, who loves and supports everyone. We are born imperfect, and we thrive to improve, but too egoistic to admit. We all do it, hating someone for their accent, clothing, opinion, and achievements. But the good thing is, it shows a maturity that we can control ourselves, from not starting to yell at that one cousin in the family gathering or that one mutual friend.

Now, look at someone who passes mean, insensitive comments. Why does someone hate? They themselves are mentally in such a bad condition, they get least bothered by their ethics and morals, which we might call a formality. Just because they feel their identity is somewhat hidden.

We live in a memes world, where people have magnifying glasses to just find someone who made a mistake or did something embarrassing to make memes out of it. There is a fine line and good and bad in everything. But I have seen people, just because they think someone said something wrong, or they don't like someone, or that someone may be controversial. In pursuit of making someone "happy", we emotionally bully someone else. Now I am not talking about every meme page, but this phenomenon exists. I have seen one of my friends, who is partially relevant, being accused of something and then being made fun of.

This is not just for memes, how often we see any celebrity or any person doing something "problematic" and we see dozens of articles on them. Here is where the true problem starts, just because they show their pretended to be perfect version doesn't mean they actually angels. Give people their space, once I saw this very furious article on how cats are apparently lactose intolerant, and this one singer was feeding her cat milk and how cruel he is.

The cutest part is, we are people who promote roasting culture, we are people who "cancel" each other, we make diss tracks, we grow all these types of stuff and then we cry about being given hate. Even if you see someone as problematic, although I don't get who you call "problematic" and how we assume he/she will stay that throughout their lives. Secondly, even if someone did something dirty, shouldn't you file a complaint against them rather than making them viral. Until they make a public apology or quit, as that blushes our ego and makes us the social justice warriors?

I myself have been wrongly accused of literally nothing . And let's be honest, there are two ways to deal with a crime/wrong done by someone. Firstly, get the authorities intact, secondly, convincing them privately to avoid doing what they are doing, and let it go. What we guys do is, literally mentally torture someone to their last point, under the supreme banners of **JUSTICE, EQUALITY, AND LOVE.** Who gave us the right to say bad about anyone or anything? Who are we? On one hand, we talk about extremism and how people should take authorities in their own hands, on the other hand, we gang up on people, to emotionally ruin them, as it somehow blushes our ego and our imaginary thoughts of being a rightful "activist".

I literally have seen someone lecture people on how they become "extremist" over a case of proven blasphemy. But she, on the other hand, was literally bullying someone because of his opinion against K-Pop.

All of that being said, by haters I DO NOT MEAN, character assasination, blackmailing or online harassments of any sorts. All of these things are just the desperation of the mind and the darkness of the soul. This being social media, we have seen the holy sites being prohibited for the other gender in the time period of Umar Bin Khatab (ra) due to cases of potential harassment. That does not justify the act, my intention is not to justify it as well. It just when the mind is polluted, the garbage would spread in as many ways as possible.

We need to learn the ethics and moral values of social media before we start using it and with "we" I mean the whole society. We need to practice, tolerance and respect. I swear Allah wouldn't make you accountable for not commenting on that one picture of that "influencer" but Allah would surely hold you accountable, if that one comment of yours made her distance herself from religion or made her feel small or even pathetic. Just because you can hide behind a screen does not mean, your actions do not have consequences. A joke for you, can be a living hell for somebody else. GROW UP.

The Ramification

The thing which worries me the most is, due to social media people have and are constantly losing the art of staying patient and consistent. How many times do you see a friend or a cousin hitting the gym for the very first day and after sharing a story with the hashtag "no pain no gain", the very next week you see them quitting the gym, due to so and so excuse.

Social media instills upon a person the desire of Instant Gratification. The desire of the mind to get approval, validation, and relevance. That too, instantly. What it does is limit a person's potential and poisons the patience. How often do you see a person making two/three videos very passionately?

But after getting not much gratification, they just quit.

Right now I am writing a book. I am halfway through it and I am yet to make any post on my socials to get my "followers" know. I didn't even hint them, why? Because not only do I want to focus on the process but I also want to distill the craving of instant gratification inside me.

Likewise, I know one thing with experience, instant gratification can never help you in creating a dream work.

Or else I would have been posting screenshots every day, on how amazingly I wrote this paragraph and how "deep" I am. Why?

Because of my craving for validation that is caused due to the pleasure I received from Dopamine. When that happens.

Insecurity

How often do we look at someone and we feel, damn we can do better than them or how did they get so many followers? There are two types of jealousies, the inferior jealousy, and the rebellious jealousy. Now, I see Kylie Jenner with all her following and luxuries in life. There are two types of reactions I would have inside my mind. First, oh man, she is so beautiful and blessed. Damn that makeup brand she's wearing, oof that sassy look. Secondly, oh well, she is all fake. Look at the making up she is pulling on.

Not only are they both a form jealous but they both are extremely toxic for you as a person. As there is a limit to a person, on which they can absorb the negativity. The same negativity turns into the frustration a "hater" has and is going through. See it through this way, the constant comparing and excess of negative thinking. Again and again, can you feel the frustration, the anxiety and exhaustion a person might go through? Realizing he is not good enough, he is not cool enough, he is not relevant enough?

Not only affect you mentally, but this idea of a global world in actuality also pushes you further away in a box of your own. One thing I faced myself and I felt really ashamed of that fact was, not a long ago. I didn't know how to talk to my family. I remember typing long, long paragraphs to mother on WhatsApp. I don't know if anyone of you can relate to me or not, but that is the best example of how we start to connect with the people in front of us through the data network. Just an example of social anxiety all of us have. I will talk about social anxiety in the next chapter.

"They come home from school and they are on their devices, a whole generation is more anxious, more fragile, more depressed. They're much else comfortable taking risks. This is a real change in a generation"

"There services are killing people and causing people to kill themselves" Tim Kendall (former president of pintrest)

A Message for "Influencers"

My respected fellow creators or as you guys like to call yourself "influencers". I understand receiving PR and further helping the brand reach more people, to contribute to a country's economy and the employment rate is truly a noble cause. I myself want to be this "noble" sometimes. It's fun to receive packages and most of us have done genuine hard work to get to this point in life, and I wish everyone nothing but success.

But every action has a consequence, modeling nice clothes or making the makeup industry a 500 US billion dollars' worth industry. As someone with any sort of influence, we need to be vigilant enough to realize. There are people, who do not have the perfect shade, there are people who do not have a perfect figure, and there are people who cannot afford the brand you are wearing. Your intentions might not be wrong, but there is someone out there watching you so pretty and "perfect" feeling pity for herself. Feeling bad and jealous of the privilege you have.

Now you cannot care about any of this, but at least be honest with yourself and your job. Do we deserve to call ourselves "influencers" if the only influence we bring is to feed someone insecurity? Or are we ourselves enslave to the unknown screen. Enjoying, the dopamine hits and being controlled by a few graphic designers in Silicon Valley. We should really define our roles and goals, before we crave for free stuff or followers. We are not just earning money or enjoying our way around the specific application but we are actually "influencing" the mindsets of a whole generations. It's like a snowball effect trying to manipulate our mind and behaviors and we all are addicted and promoting it. Stop promoting "self-love" to buy the new makeup accessory box, help people grow and develop themselves.

Summary

Now, as a social media consumer. We are addicted to it. Not unintentionally, but through proper planning and strategy. To this extent, even the "Trigger Warning" content you see, is a way to get you to consume more and more, watch more ads. And make their pockets warmer and warmer.

Something I have done and I still do which has brought my 4-hour screen time to less than an hour is. Firstly, I have turned off the notifications of all the major applications. Except for the messaging app, as it can be important sometimes. It's not easy, but being aware of the planning I know notification is the most successful pull back strategy after complimentary food. Most people ask me why didn't you validate our post or deliver feedback on them. Firstly if you are someone, who actually focuses on who "liked" your post and who left you on seen. Quite frankly, I have been there. Then my friend, the desire of validation is not a desire anymore but an addiction. And just like any harmful desire, it will only pollute your mindset.

Secondly, I have set for myself a low

Information diet. One of the biggest fears social media instills upon a person is the fear of missing out. But, my friend you do not need to know about anything and everything. As I said earlier, life is scarce if you keep on just getting information, careless of it being useless or not. You wouldn't have enough time to implement it or share it. And it works both ways, as a creator and a consumer, I have seen so many creators milking content out of an unwilling self, just because they are afraid they might miss out on the audience they have. And they may get irrelevant, that is true as well to some extent. But shows how temporary and deceiving the platform can be.

So how does the low Information diet works, well depending on the platform you set a limit of posts, videos, and articles you go through at one time. And one the set number is completed, you ignore the next video or post. No matter how amazing and relatable the thumbnail may sound.

It's an infinite loop, created with machine learning of millions of dollars investment. Your every next video would be more interesting than the first one because, as I said earlier it all works on the Attention Economy. They want your attention as much as possible. Reminds of that ayah from Quran, "Indeed, mankind is in loss" (103-2). The man who rejects and questions God and its greatest reasons. Is enslaved and controlled by an application in a gadget. We were scared of robots and AI to kill us or backfire, do we realize it already has started?

Thirdly, realize if someone is hating you, that's the lack of validation and the level of insecurity a person is going through. But that does not mean the element of respect should ever be lost.

Unit #3

RELATIONSHIPS

CHAPTER #1

THE NEED

We as human beings are born as social animals, we need company, we need help, we need shelter and care. No matter how much we present the idea of self-love, we are created in pairs and in groups. We do require, humanly support, validation, and affection. Even shown through research feral kids, the human beings born and raised in forests have found parents and friends in animals. As proudly, we feed ourselves, we are independent. The reality is we are not independent, we are dependent on other human beings, and we are affected by other human beings. Socially, economically and emotionally. We are interdependent in everything in our lives, for example, no matter how brilliant we are or how amazing our certain product is. If we wouldn't have any consumers, how do you think you or your product would grow?. Similarly, you are having meetings every day, you make a fortune, living in a cool residence, traveling around the world and you hear, your loved one just passed away, wouldn't you be affected by that? So the idea we sell ourselves, of being independent is a bullsh*t. The matter of fact is, in order to survive we need to have good relationships, and to have good relationships we need to understand a few things. In the twenty-first century, we live in the world, in which networking is the key to success and growth. And if we keep in mind these basic principles we would have control over how we can make healthy bonds and how they might work.

Humans are weird

Keep this in your mind and apply this to every relationship you know and have in life. It will help you and your relationship with anyone respectively to grow, stay together, and be positive. Remember, humans are born imperfect, born to make blunders. There is no such thing as a good person or a bad person, just bad or good decisions, timings, and influence. Someone you dislike is as capable of doing a great thing as much as someone you admire to make a blunder. Life is that way, there is a reason why it's a testing ground. There is a reason why even being so physically, mentally, emotionally even financially desiring of each other. We are each other's biggest, enemy, obstacle, and haters.

Isn't it weird though, we care about the opinion of others to a level we do not hesitate sacrificing our dreams, why? Because people might not like it and on the other hand we backbite and dislike the same people. It's like, I dislike Islamophobist but on the same hand, I would stop practicing Islam publicly. Like, what are you trying to do? Get the clarity of mind, if you love them then accept them. If you hate them, the stop worrying about their opinions!!

Anyhow, firstly, stop making these fancy labels in your mind, oh he is a good guy and the next day tweeting against him for some blunder he/she might have done. What it does is, it makes this expectation back of mind about the person, of how amazing, great, and in a way perfect they are. What it does is, it either makes you disappointed and bad about the person, when they make a mistake or you literally start worshipping them becoming blind on anything they do. These are the two extremes we see in our society, either we worship someone or we just hate him. Again, that's both connected with your thinking and your emotions. That's why I emphasized so much early on, with different types of emotions and different perspectives on them. There is a reason why the rule of God goes like, a good deed erases the bad one. Similarly, what you may find good, the other may find wrong. What you may find wrong, others may find good. There isn't any rule book imprinted on the surface of the earth. And we have seen the words of Divine been manipulated by the man, to their own benefit. Complex I tell you. Now you might give me examples of a murderer or a rapist, that how can I say there aren't any bad people and what would I call them, well, firstly if your mind connected to this example know you are reading this book in the rebellious denial phase, looking for excuses to disagree and prove me wrong. This brings me to another point, stop looking at people with the eyes and ears to point them out wrong or to disagree with them. And to your assumed question, sucide is an act, is a bad choice. But you cannot say the person was "bad". That being said, that act led to him reaching an end in this world and if you believe in the other world you know better what might happen there. Acts like these multiply the whole of the life's work to zero, but then again it's the bad decision not the bad person, as a mother does not create a "bad person" neither does Allah. But the wrong decisions.

"Listen to understand rather disagree"

As I said it's our subconscious instinct to feel suspicious about the wrong, but always listen with fresh ears and think without a bias-free mind, having a bias-free mind is inevitable but one should try their best.

Similarly, you just cannot judge a person. For example, at this exact moment, I am writing this book on my phone, my parents and everyone around would have no clue whatsoever, on what I am doing. They might be thinking, I am texting someone or I am wasting my time playing my game. Do understand, you judge with respect to your own experiences and teachings, for example, if you use the phone mostly for texting and gaming and so does all the people around you. You would automatically assume someone using their phone is doing one of the two. Given you an on the spot example of judging/assuming wrongly. This shows how big of a problem assuming can be, how many times have we seen a very healthy and peaceful marriage been jeopardized by simply an assumption we make in our minds, simply due to some experience we have witnessed or we know has happened in the society. It's not the interrogation that's harmful but the doubt and lack of trust. Take your time, process the situation before you make any judgments, as regret is the father of wrong actions.

The reality of the matter is, we as humans do wrong unintentionally as well as intentionally, and no one of us is created the same way. Our minds are different from each other, appearance even something as small as a fingerprint is different from each other. But saying that, "we are a some of five closed ones in our lives" we despite being different adapt from each other"

Here are some things we need to do in order to have better friendships and healthy relationships.

Learn to Validate

As I talked about validation, in the earlier chapter. Validation is one of the most refreshing and strengthening ways to grow a bond. Every relationship in the world desires appreciation, a sense of belonging, and a good vibe coming from the other end. From a student to an employee, from a son to spouse. From parents to friends. Let me go in deep, why do we praise Allah, while communicating with him? Does he have the validation? Or is it a cognitive behavior when you compliment someone wholeheartedly and honestly, the affliction with that someone increases within. Similarly, it's a habit we are taught through prayers and a very powerful relationship lesson. That whenever you want anything from someone, whether it may be financially, emotional or physical help. Learn to appreciate, before requesting. And when you request someone something, have it in you to clear the hearts before you ask anything.

How often do we appreciate the people close to us in life? Our siblings, parents, close friends?

Learn to appreciate and respect the relationships in front of you, near you. As it only creates mutual respect but defuses the negativity of the mind.

The Area Of Dispute

The real dispute between two human beings starts when the diversity factor creeps in when the whole aspect of right and wrong. Truth and lie come to the play. As for me, Believe in One God is a right, but for an atheist, the same statement can be wrong. Everyone believes, their beliefs are the righteous truth, including me. The reality is, truth is something only the divine knows all we have is interpretations. Someone might believe the earth is flat that's true for him, but we obviously disagree. Similarly, except for a few facts, most humans accept the facts. Something very interesting in this perspective is an opinion, once I was invited to a podcast with my Co-host. He was like how the elders at times have wrong "opinions". At that very point, something struck me and I genuinely believe it.

The opinion is never written of wrong, no one has an opinion that is "wrong" in their heads. An opinion cannot be right or wrong, as every opinion is based upon a person's experience, limited understanding, and customs, a person is brought up in. So that opinion, applying to your life is a different thing. It being "wrong" is a totally different thing.

The most destructive dispute among the masses is the dispute of difference of opinion. We hear and say, how a difference of opinion is alright and how a difference of opinion leads to growth and all that. But only if we started, to stop worshipping our opinions, more than opinions ourselves. Which further

Once we get beyond that, we come to realize there

are more perspectives and ways of looking at things than one. Which further brings us to peace, while we think of a difference of opinion and further respect.

Understand, Allah is the acquirer of the greatest of knowledge, there are new researches and new enhancements every day in every field and have been going on for centuries. From the complex human mind to a rock. The studies have been here for ages yet there is no starting or ending to them. Thus why always remember even if you are lucky and wise enough to crack a code, a way or a perspective. Realize, the possibilities and ways Allah has created are definitely more than one. And it is possible, the other person may look at something from a perspective bigger than yours. So, never reject any opinion, listen, question, think, analyze, and if you do not feel comfortable will it, stay with your own. But, have the respect as long as the person can stick to their own opinion. As the knowledge of Allah is infinite and so are the possibilities. We only know bits or even anything else. If there was one way of life or one answer to a question, you wouldn't be here in this world. Likewise, if you do not agree with me or couldn't understand me, doesn't mean I am wrong!

Expectations

"Too many expectations on someone else's shoulder can be a burden to yourself"

Now I won't tell you not to expect, because that would be the easiest and the most naive thing to say as the expectation is again a human instinct. But what I will tell you is to be wise with what you are expecting and why you are expecting that. With keeping in mind that the other person is fully capable of disappointing you and becoming mentally ready for it.

Benefit of Doubt

One thing that helped me connect to people on a deeper level was the art of giving the other person the benefit of the doubt. Like, what they might be saying is wrong. What they might be doing is wrong, but try to genuinely understand from their viewpoint. What and why is making them do all this. Look at people's mistakes, like it's your parents or your children or even your idol who has done the mistake. And look at the angle, how you would try defending them. In order to truly connect with someone and have genuine empathy and respect. Benefit of doubt is a learnable attribute which we all should apply in our lives. Someone once asked me how to make friends and more importantly how to not lose the old ones. I replied with one phase and four words; benefit of doubt. What is the benefit of doubt? The state of accepting something/someone as honest or deserving of trust even though there are doubts (google)

The Golden Rule

It is found in traditional psychology, no matter how self-satisfied and nice, you are to yourself. There is always a door or a window that is left untouched. Scientists researched on why some monk's meditation and wearing few clothes are more self-satisfied than some of the millionaires. With deeper analyses, they found the science of human belonging. No matter how healthy, wealthy, or sufficient we are. There is peace and satisfaction, a person who never is able to feel, for who doesn't give back to the community.

"The community doesn't need you, you need them"

The happiness and joy you get when are aware of how you made someone else happy are outrageous. And that is the true way, how you gain peace and send positive vibes back to the community. This one rule in life, never fails. This universal law is found in different terminologies in different scripts, but the point is the same. The Golden rule that never fails; the rule of providing love and service to others, while understanding you are no one.

The happiness and joy you get when are aware of how you made someone else happy are outrageous. And that is the true way, how you gain peace and send positive vibes back to the community.

"Help one another in acts of piety and righteousness. (5-2)

"And do not forget to do good and to share with others, for with such sacrifices God is pleased". (Hebrews 13:16)

Charity given out of duty, without expectation of return, at the proper time and place, and to a worthy person is considered to be in the mode of goodness (Gita)

"The community doesn't need you, you need them"

"The purpose of life is not to be happy. It is to be useful, to be honorable, to be compassionate, to have it make some difference that you have lived and lived well" (Ralph Waldo Emerson)

Let your selfishness dive into the purity of providing services to others and thereby enjoy the key to the purpose, peace and happiness.

In short, if you learn to listen to someone genuinely, validate them honestly, tolerate them, and respect them. You would be able to make a formidable bond with anyone and everyone.

"Always grow a tree, where you don't have the shadow to sit under".

Sensitive Point

There is a triggering point to everyone, regardless of their calmness and composure. Whether it maybe about the culture, family, religion or even the country or community. We all get triggered and explode, to a limit. It's not always about being extremist rather being sensitive about a certain issue or topic, as team certain, we should ensure to not blow up on someone who does not deserve it, likewise we should RESPECT. Respect is the only thing with trust that a bond or a relationship truly needs.

Respect people and be respected, as simple as that. **Understand division in communities is the point from where the growth is truly neglected.**

CHAPTER #2

PARENTAL

The most essential yet complicated relationship. Yet most of us are not in a very healthy relationship with our parents. It took me three and a half years to crack, why parents are so bossy, why they don't understand us, why don't they just support us.

Well, the bossy because they pay your bills, as simple as that. It's weird, how we forget the fact just because they love us or rather they have the "responsibility" and expectations in our head to love us unconditionally, which I am sure they already do. But that doesn't take away the fact they work their ass off, to put a roof on our head and food in our stomach, learn to be grateful.

Just remember, most often than not your parents try their best to think about your betterment according to their own understanding of life. Which by the way, can never be refused or dejected.

In this relatively small chapter, I will try to give you perspectives on how you can revive your relationship with your parents. I myself, try working on all this stuff as I ain't a great son myself.

One thing about this relationship is time, when you want them, they are here but when they want you, you are busy building your empire.

Now coming to the point, why don't they understand you. Firstly, this is such a selfish and careless approach to life. When you wait for someone to make an assumption about you and they are actually being right about it. Also, why do you expect anyone to understand you when you don't understand them? When did you try to understand them, their thinking, and their decisions? Like, you expect them to know when you are happy, when you are sad. You expect them to agree to everything you say, you want actions from them but are too botherless to even give them words.

Remember what goes around comes around, especially in this matter. They are most probably treated the way they are treating you. Or every action has an equal or opposite reaction. They might treat you totally differently. Once a person texted me, my dad is super nice and all but he can be toxic sometimes, I shouldn't tell you this but he does not hesitate hitting my mother. I get traumatized, scared and angry. I asked him to do three things, firstly, talk to your mother, and give her love and respect. Tell her, you are here for her and she is no stranger to hard times. There was a catch, as I told him, I would only tell you the second when you finished with the first and third when you finished with the second task. He agreed to my condition, and he was like; "well nothing wrong in trying another technique". I at the end triggered his ego, a little by saying; "I don't think you can"

Anyhow, He texted me back, "bro, I am done with the first part. It was done very smoothly, never saw my mother's eyes so sparking. Now tell me the second part, I cannot wait!" I asked him to do the same with your dad. And he went completely silent, "bro, you don't know my dad, he is not like your father". Hesitant looking for excuses, I asked him, so you cannot do it can you? My reverse psychology worked and he texted, "wait for my text". I texted him, back do not forget to express to him your anxiety and sadness. And do tell him know, you know, it's hard for him but he is stronger than all of this. He texted me, a few days back. "Bro I am done and I feel so bad for my father, he is an amazing man, dude". "He surely would be", I replied. He told me how his mother doubts his father on a rumor she heard, and how his financial life is going through a crisis.

I told him, time for the last task huh? He was ready, I asked him to take your parents out for dinner. Express to both of them how you feel, ask them to sort things out. Tell your mother, to stop believing everything she hears. And tell your father, to stop taking the frustrations out on them, in a very casual and sarcastic way. So their ego does not get hurt.

He texted me again a few days later. "Man, I feel so relaxed and calm after doing the final task". I wished him luck and prayers for the future. Then after almost six weeks, after he texted me. I was like to myself, "damn man, I think that did not work". With that in my mind, I opened the message in which he wrote; "dude, you are a genie, you did something that even my grandparents couldn't"

You see, I can write novels as well. Anyhow, a few lessons we can all take to our life are; Firstly, Mommy and Daddy are as human as any of us. Just because they try to stay composed in front of us doesn't mean, they are emotionless or everything is alright at their end amd even they don't the human thing, their brought up and their struggle it all comes to the equation. Stop looking at everything, from your perspective. In fact, give them the 'benefit of doubt'. And they can f*ck up as badly as possible.

Secondly, the importance of communication. Your parents do need anything but some love and attention. Once an old man used to go to the hospital with his son. The son used to drop his father to his house, and leave for work. One day, the son was running late for his work, he asked his father to stay at his friend's office till he got free and picked him up. The son started observing his father, going every morning somewhere and not only that his reports started getting way healthier. The son got curious, he followed his father and saw him going to his friend's office. When the old man left the office, the son went in and asked his friend, what's going on man? He replied, nothing much just your father comes, I offer him some tea and he goes on and on about life and everything and all I do is listen.

My friends, communication is something most essential for this relationship yet, it's at its minimum, I am guilty of this myself. There is a world outside your insecurity and fears, let's stop being selfish and careless, about our lives and our moods. And give time to those who own it.

The relationship with parents is no less than a whole journey. With time being the dead-end of the road. Your time is sufficient and we as children forget that. We get to be involved in our lives, goals, and friendships. We almost forget our buddies, our teachers, and our partners. And I myself am guilty of all of this. Just I try, and I want all of you to try as well.

The biggest factor of hurt and pain in this relationship is, both sides expect and want the best from each other, but in the process, they forget about the relationship itself.

For example, your parents try to become the mean, from which you get shelter, food, and other necessities and wants of life. But in the same process, they forget that a child is not a robot or a vending machine, from which they insert money and get achievements in returns. It's a developing human brain, that as much as it needs shelter and food, it also needs love and support.

One of the major reasons, why from that growing

age the kids turn rebellious and deprived. And they start to avoid their parents because; firstly the adolescent brain is selfish and narrow minded, Secondly it requires a lot of encouragement and validation rather than do and don'ts all the time. It's a two way street, but that does not deny the fact we are indebted to our parents. No matter how rude or cruel they might be, we still have to respect and genuinely care for them.

"And We have enjoined on man (to be good) to his parents. In travail upon travail did his mother bear him, and in two years was his weaning. Show gratitude to Me and to thy parents; to Me is thy final goal." (Quran 31:14)

According to the above verse, gratitude to God and parents go hand in hand. Gratitude to God is incomplete without showing gratitude to one's parents. Since being grateful to God is a form of ibadah (worship) that earns heavenly rewards, it can therefore be said that being grateful to one's parents also earns heavenly rewards.

"We have enjoined on man kindness to his parents; in pain did his mother bear him, and in pain did she give him birth." (Quran 46:15)

Thus, God has enjoined us to show kindness, respect, and humility to our parents. We are commanded to do this, even though they may have injured us. The only exception to the above command is made in the following verse:

"We have enjoined on man kindness to his parents; but if they strive (to force) thee to join with Me anything of which thou hast no knowledge, obey them not." (Quran 29:8)

Some of the traditions of Prophet Muhammad, and of the learned members of his family, about our responsibilities toward our parents are quoted here:

"He who wishes to enter Paradise through its best door must please his parents."

CHAPTER #3

"RELATIONSHIPS"

As temporary as this topic is in the context of our book. Yet I have to discuss it because we all have either been through it or desired to be in it or simply are in it. I still don't get why we call it "relationship" it should rather be called "the unnecessary overly complicated friendship". Now jokes aside this is one of the most relatable issues, and to our luck, it is indirectly connected with our topic and it's definitely the need of the hour.

Now we see different patterns and perspectives in different types of relationships, so this chapter being the most relatable might be unrelated at times, so bear with me.

Now being a life coach, the question and problem I am asked the most are about this very topic. So I will start off by saying, no relationships ain't cool.

Also, if your relationship only has love, my friend

you have a perfect script of a Bollywood movie with a slow sad song in the background. But, that's not loving, I am not denying love. Just that the idea of love we have, is too early to be seen through now. Now don't tell me about love at first sight, because I as a believer believe in love my God without seeing him directly. And dislike Trump no matter how much I see him. So love doesn't need any sights, to begin with.

This is a rather short chapter and summary, as we all suffer through it and it can be a real enemy to our purpose of consciousness.

I am gonna divide this chapter into further three categories. Pre, Present, and Post. With respect to your status and problem. Although, relationships have so many streams and possibilities. I will try to keep it short and universal.

Post Relationship

This is a hard time, as we humans hurt more than ever we love. Whatever the reason might be, I am not here to consolidate with you or anything. Neither am I a "relationship advisor" but once you stop feeding yourself, how pure love was, or listening to "bewafa" songs and feeling pity for yourself or why the other person didn't stay. There is no, specific way to come out of this phase, time surely helps a lot. Healing takes time, just feed yourself hope and growth.

I will not give you a lecture on "self-love" or "self-importance" you probably have heard all of that. Just remember, "all the wonders you seek and within yourself" it all starts from the mind and it all ends from there. The heart is just the expression of the soul and the byproduct of your thinking. Your heart is the indicator of your desire, all the lust you feel, all the moods you have, it's all possessed through the thinking of the brain, felt by the heart. (I will dive deep, into the philosophy of heart in the last chapter)

The Rule Of Rejection

My friend, remember rejections are normal. You reject people, people reject you, that's how life works. Regardless of your skill, personality, and your probability, you will get rejected in life. And you will reject a lot of people yourself. From a salesperson to someone who might like you, but you don't like them. From someone who texted you to someone whom you texted. Remember how I told you to say "no", well in this case, learn to say "okay" as well, someone hurted you? Oh well, okay! Someone wants to break up with you? "Okay". Do not make things complicated for no reason, it's a free world, as long as they are not harming your privacy or you 'physically', let it be.

We as humans are born with a tendency to hurt each other. Intentionally, unintentionally. To people we love, to people, we do not like. In fact, we hurt people we love more than the people we dislike. Due to our love and expectations from them.

It's all about realization and moving on. The more you play the victim to how you loved them, how you did this for them, how you did that, that's only just fueling your pain and getting pleasure from it.

The Urge to Change

Change is essential, People change, their priorities change, their dreams change, their mindsets change and their surroundings change. Never fear change, but adapt to it as with change and time does the realities reveal, with time the emotions grow or change. And with time, a person gets closer and closer to reality.

So people will change, you have changed. Look at your post from three years ago, don't you feel grown up and mature? That's how life is, change is the essentiality that keeps the existence,

Living. Or else, what would be a difference between a mountain and a person?

"Grief does not change you, Hazel. It reveals you" John Green

If you are in a relationship, know your partner will change, not only partner but friend, siblings, hell your life! It would all change, from your face to your mind.

"Nothing can resist the change until the change resist them"

The Art of Timing

Damn, I am covering some really cool concepts here. **"They plan, And Allah plans and indeed Allah is the best of planners" (3-54)**

"You are, where you meant to be" (not mine)

Stay calm and realize, you are not ahead of you, certainly not behind. You choose, the way with your own will, and it is your own will that makes you unique and stands out, but if you have the courage and strength to accept it. You chose to be with that specific someone and it's you, who feel bad for yourself.

Everything happens for a reason at the right time, it's not only the hardship but a hardship at the time, you need to learn from it the most. Think about it, if the lessons you learned at the peak ages of your life. If you would've learned them, at a younger age. Would it have had any impact? Similarly, we truly genuinely learn a lesson, when we feel it. There are a hundred videos on YouTube, A thousand books, and millions of people with hardships and pain, the lessons we truly feel and learn are the ones we felt directly or indirectly. Everything is going according to the timing. Think about it, if you lecture a five year old kid about lust, do you think he would understand shit? Similarly, how many times we have heard, relationships are the worst, they dumb, etc. Yet we tried on our own to come to the conclusion. Ever wondered, why it happens? Feelings, you only understand something when you feel it. Whether it be a lecture on lust or relationships. You are telling a ten year old kid how hard it is to earn money. Do you think he will understand up until he feels and himself directly or indirectly.

Similarly, the lesson you learnt was there for you to learn, you just wanted to feel it to connect deeply and truly. And it was all part of a plan, a plan most certainly greater than ours.

The Toxic use of Expressions

Listen to this very carefully, I myself someone who enjoys and craves a little philosophy and deeper perception. But my friends, all of these lines such as "my heart broke" are just an expression of pain, not the reality.

People literally give me examples like, "just the way glass can never be glued back to the same position that's how my heart is shattered into pieces". And I look at that message and just stare at it. If you want to talk deep, poetic. It's fine, but stop giving real-life examples to follow your claim and further build a whole storyline on it. On how your heart broke and everything in between.

My friends, we take these "expressions" too seriously. The heart is made of flesh and blood, you can never "break" it. Even if you throw it or drop it. It stays in the same form, and that is what the true philosophy of heart is, no matter how much pain or how big of the hardship, it can never break a man's heart.

These dumb expressions, #brokenheartposts, and illusionary of a dream world. Are all bullshit, you need to become aware of.

All of this stuff contributes to a bigger level, and affects your emotional and mental well-being. Learn to say "no" to whatever tragedy happened to you, no as in I won't submit to you. Your pain and struggle can be very hard, but I'll tell you a story of a Sahabiyah (female companion) who lost her brother, father, and husband in the battle of Uhud. When she was told, all her loved ones died, the first question she asked was Is my Prophet alive?" Take me to him as he is my only will to live".

You can be hurt, you will be hurt. But the real heart never breaks, up until you cut it out. And that is the philosophy of a heart, it's not meant to be broken.

Before entering the relationship

This is the most controllable stage among all, I know you are young. It's most probably your first time, or maybe you think you found your lucky one. Maybe it's your crush or maybe she's the cutest girl of the school or town.

Before you get too excited, calm your dopamine and question yourself. Why do you want to be in a "relationship"? What good will it do to both of your life? What is your goal with this relationship and how do you plan on achieving that goal? Lastly, why do you "need" to be in a relationship?

Now, the answers would be different for everyone and from everyone. But if you want to be in a relationship because you "like" or "love" that specific person then don't bother. In fact, become friends with someone, with the intention to stay friends rather than look for an opportunity to strike.

Breakup a New Starting

A breakup is never the ending, but the starting. The start of a newer and improved you. With a hurt ego which made you think that one person would stay. You feel broken and dead from the inside. You feel lonely and pointless. But only if the man knew, it's the love which is selfish and in order to restrain it. We need to analyze it.

That being said, "Change" is something that truly helps with rewiring yourself. From changing the haircut to your status, it's the small changes in your physical appearance that helps your mental stereotypes.

Lastly, I really made a mess of the topic as it's too detailed to dive into, but if I dive into it I would lose the trueness of the topic, but one thing which is really common and something we should all be "conscious" about is.

The Desire of Rebound

After being rejected or after breaking up with someone. There is human behavior, which is really toxic to society. So, once you reach the rebellious and angry phase of post-relationship status. In which, people tend to do really ugly stuff, from blackmailing to bullying. In that same phase, the person feels the urge of loneliness but on the same hand, feeds himself "he is better than her". People tend to find new partners just for their temporary desire and after that phase, they come to realize they never were interested in the person. So they simply ghost them or start ignoring them. That leaves another totally innocent person hurt for no reason at all.

Few universal tips:

Keep your relationship free from three things and you can achieve some sort of certainty. 1. Respect more than you love, 2. Keep third party influence away (stop involving friends in your relationships, respect privacy) 3. Integrity over emotions. No matter how hurt or overwhelmed you might be self-respect is always better than begging or being creepy.

CHAPTER # 4

EXERCISES

H ere are a few tips and techniques on how you can improve your relationships with anyone.

1. Talk to Listen

Whenever you talk to somebody, talk in a manner to listen and understand to the other person, and stop the desire of the mind to disagree at everything.

2. Hear to understand

Whenever you listen to any perspective or opinion, listen in a manner you actually try to understand it. Rather than look for points to disagree.

3. Validate

Appreciate, and compliment the other person's importance in your life. And let them know, they belong here.

4. Forgive

Always, have the courage to forgive someone. If you are ready to accept and tolerate them in your life.

UNIT #4

SPIRITUAL ESSENCE OF LIFE

CHAPTER #1

INTRODUCTION TO THE ALMIGHTY

I have been preaching "control" from the beginning. I myself practice control and it has helped me a lot in almost every aspect of life. The reason I am sharing with you is, my journey to self-control started from here,

I was hesitant for this chapter at first, as people may misunderstand the chapter to something religious, but I thought maybe I should name it this way. As people need an introduction to God Almighty, not because they do not know who He is, just we confuse God to certain groups, parties and people. So here is an Introduction to God and why He is essential, and the constant of the equation of existence.

This isn't an argument or evidence. It's my perspective, analysis, and thought that helped my vision and perspective grow. As growing up, we all have read and heard about all the beautiful and tremendous Attributes that Allah Almighty has, we know them yet we are unaware of them. I am not here to tell you, who Allah is, rather I am here to share with you why we need Allah. The most near to us, yet someone we try to go most far from. The ever-living and the ever merciful, without his permission doesn't a leaf fall. He is the light of the hearts and the love of the soul. To him, we all follow and to him, we are all accountable. One free from all worldly needs and desires, all hearer and the all-seeing. Closer than the self, beyond all the existence.

I want to have a heart to heart dialogue with you. This chapter will bring a fresh perspective to that I have said earlier. This will be the most powerful and difficult unit to write, not because I don't have anything to write but because I have a lot to write and I need to concise it and put it in a reader-friendly and touching manner.

Once an atheist asked me, how do you know if there exists a God? This is a question, which has almost infinite answers yet no textbook or "right" answer so to say. What I replied to him was, **"I don't want to get into if God exists or not what I**

know is, I exist and I exist only because of the thought back of my mind that God exists"

Think about it, all the injustice in the world, all the lack of equality, and the lack of equity. But how do we survive? Once, an old poor man who did not have any assets, any assistants. Lost all his family is a murder case, a young man came to him and asked him. Oh, old man, what is the purpose of your living, you barely can walk. You have no support system or any help, how would you survive? He replied with just one word "Allah". Why is their hope inside us whenever something unfair happens to us, that God is watching? Who do we turn to when we come to understand we are powerless, we are insufficient and egos were just a fraud? Who is our last resource? Stuck in the middle of the sea, with hunger and poverty whom will we call upon other than you Almighty?

You might not believe in Allah or the hereafter, or you might call his justice as "karma" or the law of nature but, the reality is we as humans need a force, energy or entity above us to rescue us, protect us and bring justice. And the spiritual certainty starts with the connection with the True Certain (Allah) which is free from change, growth or death.

Why does someone suicide? They get tired, they get fed up, they get hopeless or they just get exposed to the reality of life and they just do not have Allah to fall back too. Someone who suicides isn't weak. In fact, they are smart, they are smart to understand the reality of this world. As Allah says in the Quran repeatedly, the world of this life is nothing but an illusion, delusion, and even "deceiving enjoyment". They not weak, they just didn't bother connecting with The Almighty as they were busy feeding their "self"

Allah is the need, I talked earlier about how your mind is the dictator of your ground. I talked at the beginning of the chapter how my control and patience started from here. Let me explain to you what I meant, the self-control started when I realized, I am nothing!

"All the power you have is in realizing you are nothing"

After getting the news of Haj, that with the Will of Almighty. I would be performing pilgrimage this year, I started doing my research on what to do and how to do it. In the process, I got so into "myself" I started being this jerk with my friends. I started making them feel small with my egoistic talks. Do you know a very interesting thing? I used to reflect inside myself even back then if I am doing anything wrong or not and I used to find nothing, because of this idea of self-love in my mind, and I am being dead honest here.

With the same mindset, I went to Makkah. And for the very first time, I was standing in front of the Kabbah surrounded by thousands of people. I realized, the moment of truth, the hard way. I am nothing, but I am everything if I have you along, Oh Allah.

At that very moment, I understood the Allah Equation. No matter what value you have on the other end, no matter how much money, power, or influence. If someone has Allah on his side, that scale would be heavier.

Self-awareness, self-evaluation, and control is something I advocate myself. You are only able to reflect upon yourself when you are free from the bias to love yourself. As humans, we have a tendency to love the perfect and dislike the imperfect, how often do we distance ourselves from a friendship with someone over something you find disgusting in them? Similarly, it's really very hard to love the self and be unbiased evaluating it. If you love it, then you become blind about it. With all due respect to everyone, but as far as I am concerned self-love isn't the answer to every problem a person goes through. In fact, there is a difference between being comfortable with yourself, being grateful for who you are and how you are and actually being crazy about yourself.

Self-love neglects the idea of self-awareness. As Imam Al Ghazali said, **"The biggest idol a person worships is the self**

For me, it was the guidelines by God and the love of God that inspired me to be a better person (Again it's a constant battle on becoming better and staying that).

So yeah, for me love doesn't start from the self. Because if it starts from there, it will stay there. And you will come to a point in life, where you may start to dislike everything other than yourself. Just like in my case, I made this assumption I am very special and started to look down upon my friends. It all started loving myself.

This was where for me I started finding (and still

finding) the answers with having Allah in my life. I learned to be grateful, for whatever I am and how I am. I saw my shortcomings, I saw my bad habits rather than hiding them from excuses. And I learned the true essence of love, which is nowhere near what we consider it as.

You see, Allah isn't just the protector or the savior, He is also a guider. Anyhow, continuing my journey, after self-evaluation I recognized the need of Allah, and after having Allah in my life. I found hope and possibility, the possibility to fight the negativity, and the hope to fight against fears and hard times. The peace and calmness I discovered, I only wish to express it and spread it.

For me, Allah was the equalizer in the equation, and it very frankly gave me an advantage over others. Anyone can have this advantage, but will anyone?

Just think about how beautiful and magnificent Allah SWT is, He creates a universe. He creates man, He teaches him the use of the pen, He provides him with food and shelter from mother's womb to someone in a cave and till the last breath we take. Just to hear the man say, "Oh how independent I am and I achieved everything in life on my own"

And how poor is the situation of the man, who works twenty years in order to get his hands on a bright molded metal, how he craves so badly for love and affection in his life, how he pays fortune for therapy, how he wants to be happy? The example of the man is like, a person who genuinely craves knowledge but looks for it in pubs.

Allah is not Unfair

We all are ungrateful, we are born imperfect, selfish but we desire perfection. Allah is not unfair, just because you might not be as good looking as someone else, your life might be harder than then your friend's (which by the way, you can never be sure of) you might not be blessed with a specific blessing, but Allah would surely compensate. There is a reason, a Muslim is taught to believe in the hereafter, there is a reason, he hereafter is one of the major pillars of Islam. A Muslim is taught to believe, because;

"If you asked them, "Who created the heavens and earth and subjected the sun and the moon?" they would surely say, "Allah ." Then how are they deluded? Allah extends provision for whom He wills of His servants and restricts for him. Indeed

Allah is, of all things, Knowing. And if you asked them, "Who sends down rain from the sky and gives life thereby to the earth after its lifelessness?" they would surely say " Allah ." Say, "Praise to Allah "; but most of them do not understand. And this worldly life is not but diversion and amusement. And indeed, the home of the Hereafter - that is the [eternal] life, if only they knew". (Surah Al Ankabut)

These four consecutive ayahs, right here are perfect to understand the situation of ours. Allah SWT, clearly tells them. They would not disagree with me or my blessings. "But most of them do not understand", do not understand what? That this world is nothing but a diversion and a distraction. And Allah SWT ends the ayah with, "only if they knew" you know like the sigh of pity.

Imagine seeing a disable in higher grades of Jannah, than someone who prayed day and night. And that very moment, will we actually realize Allah was never unfair. Just this world, isn't created to be fair. It's just, we have been introduced to a different Allah altogether, On one side, He is shown to be a kind, a sweet grandpa who loves all and this life and everything you do is a joke, all fun and games. On the other side, He is shown to be a vicious creator, who likes to torture his slaves Nauzbillah.

In reality, Allah's mercy does overrule Allah's wrath but that doesn't mean you live a rebellious life. And expect him to give you the same place, He would give someone, who fought his desires for Allah in this world of illusion and pleasure. Just remember the higher the sacrifice, the greater the reward. That being said, even in this world If Allah doesn't give you something or you lack something, that doesn't mean you lost. Allah always compensates with an increase in something else. Stop racing the horses in the sea and complaining about your luck. The best example I can give you is of Stephen Hawking. Despite all the infections being paralyzing, he understood his extraordinary capacity given with brains. The compensation for his infection and inability.

"Do you think that you will enter the garden while Allah has not yet known those who strive hard from among you, and (he has not) known the patient". (3-142)

So in conclusion it's not Allah's justice that's questionable but your perspective and how you understand.

. The Mercy

It's Allah's mercy, that he looks for excuses to forgive you and love you. From Allah knowing the psychology of human beings, Allah SWT has used two of the biggest ways to influence a person's will. With Greed and Fear.

"Surely those who do good their place of entertainment shall be the gardens of Jannah" (18-107)

"And never think that Allah is unaware of what the wrongdoers do. He only delays them for a day when eyes will stare" (14-42)

How caring Allah SWT is, He tests us in this world, with grief, loss, poverty. Just to be able to bless us with rewards greater than illusions.

The next time you ask yourself, **why me?**

"Do people think they will be left alone after saying "we believe" without being put to test? (29-2)

"Allah tests those, who He loves more" (Hadith)

And "surely after every difficulty, there is ease" (94-5)

"but give glad tidings to the steadfast" (2-155)

Blind Trust in Allah

Blind Trust in Allah is the superpower we all want. Very honestly, this is the key to my conscious control. The trust in Allah, when someone broke my heart. I had the trust in Allah. When I was filled with fear, I had the trust in Allah. When I was in difficult times, I had Trust in Allah. When I doubt the future, the first thing that comes in my head is the trust in Allah. When I lose, I have trust in Allah. When I start a project, I have trust in Allah. When I just want to quit, it's the trust in Allah. When I am having an emotional breakdown, I trust in Allah. When I want to leave something really special to me, I do it as I have Trust in Allah. How can I do this, trust in Allah?

There is a reason why when I failed 10th grade, one of the most important exams of my life. I didn't go into depression or thought of giving up. Rather after the early shock, I gather myself. Performed the ablution (wuzu) and went to the prayer and said "As you wish, Oh my Lord".

There was a reason, while everyone was stressed and freaked out when my father was diagnosed with cancer. I stayed patient and steadfast. There is a reason I have some control and patience. I trust all

It was all due to the trust I have in Allah.

Trust in Allah is no less than a miracle, but, **"miracles happen to those, who believe in them"**

"And whoever trusts in Allah, He is sufficient for him; surely Allah attains His purpose; Allah indeed has appointed a measure for everything" (65-3)

It was the blind trust in Allah that replace a sheep with Ismail (a), it was the blind trust in Allah that provided shelter to Yusuf (a) in the stomach of a whale, it was the blind trust in Allah that turned the heat of the fire to the breeze of coolness from Musa (a). It was the blind trust in Allah, which made Musa (a) escape through the sea.

It's not that Allah wouldn't listen to you, it's just are you ready to trust him blindly? Are you ready to trust him, more than you trust your assumptions? It's the doubt of the mind that weakens up the trust in Allah. It's a potion that shouldn't be doubted, no matter how impossible the possibility maybe.

Disobeying Allah

We all are sinners, even the best among us to the worst. We all sin, with respective capability. Some sin more, some sinless. But everyone should try improving themselves.

"Your sins are your obstacles in your path to Allah"

You know what actually invites Allah's exasperation, two things, firstly advocating disobedience and wrong. Secondly, being too egoistic to admit you did wrong.

Never doubt Allah's mercy over your capacity to sin, as a summary of Hadith Qudsi "Oh my slave, if your sins reach the sky and are heavier than the earth" I'll forgive you.

I'll forgive you but the condition of forgiveness is repentance and the condition of repentance is to go in a battle against the sin you once committed. For firm repentance, we accept our wrong and detach ourselves from that habit or sin. Its okay, if it happens again, as you fought hard. But it's not okay, to expect forgiveness for something you were afraid to leave and sacrifice.

Free Will vs Predestination

This is a question we all have or we all do

struggle with. Some believe in predestination, some believe in Free Will and some deny one of them. But in actuality, there exists a free will and there exists a predestination/luck.

Let me give you examples to make you understand, so what is something that is predestined and you cannot change it. For example, you're biological parents and your date of delivery.

Likewise, in life, you have control over which path you choose, what decision you take, or which perspective you grow yourself too. For example, move your arm in the air. Didn't you do it? Similarly, growing a beard or shaving your head. They all are free will, Allah does know about it all. But none of it was predestined.

There is a third wheel to it, and that is the magnificent Knowledge of Allah. The knowledge of the unseen, the knowledge of now, the knowledge of the past, and the knowledge of the infinite future. Allah SWT knows, by his knowledge what path will you take and where will you end up. Not that, he has forced upon you the path, you would still have to yourself think and choose. But due to his magnificent Knowledge, He knows the future, the past and the present.

But if Allah knows, I am going to hell, why did He create me in the first place?

Do not confuse Allah's knowledge with predestination. Just like a role-play in a game, which path you choose is completely on you. He is the developer of the game. He knows all the possibilities and cracks. And on which path will the person choose and get what.

But that still doesn't take away the fact, you are the controller. You choose the path, he provides you, with the blessings accordingly. For example, a person gets a wage daily, the other person gets a salary monthly. Allah has set a limit to somethings that no matter which path you chose will stay the same. For example, death and rizq (food) are some things that are predestined but their way of coming can differ to which possibility you choose. For example, a person dying at the same time but one due to natural death, the second one due to a car accident.

Hard work and predestination

Does hard work increase wealth, if I work harder in my exams will I get better grades? Will I get the same grades, if I didn't study at all?

Again here comes the essential part of Allah's knowledge, Allah knew billions of years before you, that you would work hard or you wouldn't work hard. And he set the different outcomes of the different possibilities. It might be a decision you took now or that surprised your parents. But do not limit, your knowledge to Allah's knowledge.

So if I work harder, would I be rewarded more? Yes! Does everything happen due to Allah's plan? Yes!

"And with Him are the keys of the unseen treasures. None knows them but He; and he knows what is the land and the sea, and there falls not a leaf but He knows it." (6-59)

Predestination is the time you will die, the time you are born and the different possibilities created for you. Free will is your own decision on which path to choose. There isn't one possibility of life, you choose the possibility. But likewise, Allah with his brilliant knowledge, already knows what you will do and how you will do it. He has tried to influence a human brain with almost all cognitive behaviors, from greed to fear of guilt to massive love and support.

If Allah knows something bad would happen to me, why doesn't he stop it and protect me? There is a reason why Allah gave the long amount of precautions that a human rejects to listen too, as they think. They are being trapped in boundaries. Which in reality isn't the wrongest thing, yet, most of the horrifying punishments Allah SWT talks about can be itself a precaution to scare people from not doing it. As they are not the "right thing" to do, but that doesn't mean people stop doing it.

For example, a person disobeys Allah and drinks. After drinking too much, that specific person being totally unconscious of his true self or good self. Harasses the people, on the streets. Now, obviously, that person should be punished, that person will be punished in both the worlds. But what about the person about to be oppressed? Allah SWT with his massive and complete knowledge made rules that might not always be applicable but they are made to ultimately prevent us from the shadow of evil. Whether it may be through desire or bad choices.

Similarly, why doesn't Allah stop the injustice happening in the world or why doesn't He save us when he knows something bad would happen to us?

What's the point of creating a testing ground,

when it's Indeed Allah who brings law and order? How will Allah be able to recognize the culprits and the pious? Now you may ask, but Allah has the supreme knowledge. But don't forget, you have the supreme choice as well.

Those are limits set by Allah. Those who obey Allah and His Messenger will be admitted to Gardens with rivers flowing beneath, to abide therein (forever) and that will be the supreme achievement. (4-13)

In the end, We fulfilled to them Our Promise, and We saved them and those whom We pleased, but We destroyed those who transgressed beyond bounds. (21-9)

How to get closer to Allah?

"To get close to Allah, you do not need prayers. But to stay close to Allah you definitely need prayers"

You get close to Allah by simply just three things, firstly being honest, secondly being thankful, thirdly staying patient.

Now being honesty that's necessary means with your tongue or lifestyle. But, it is a state of heart that is beloved to Allah. A state of heart that keeps you candid and close to Allah, that helps you accept your wrong and "honestly" try to improve it.

"O believers, fear God and be among those who are the truthful ones" (9-119)

Similarly, by thanking I do not mean, "Allahamdulilah" we all say. But thanking in actuality is when you appreciate Allah's blessings, and try to keep them clean, like your eyes, mouth, hands, etc. Which by no means, is an easy job to do.

"Then remember Me; I will remember you. Be grateful to Me,and do not reject Me." (2-152)

"What can Allah gain by your punishment, if you are grateful and you believe? (4-147)   (look how beautifully Allah questions us and tells us. If you are grateful to me, why the hell would I punish you for?)

And lastly, patience. Patience is further divided into three categories, Patience when hardship is bestowed upon you. Patience while fulfilling the obligations and patience while protecting yourself from the unlawful.

"And Allah loves the patient" (3-146)

"Indeed, Allah is with the patient" (8-46)

CHAPTER #2

SPIRITUAL INTELLIGENCE

Spirituality can be defined as the pursuit of chasing an entity higher than any other. Everyone has a spiritual life, some feel it by meditating, some feel it by enjoying nature and some feel it by praying the traditions.

As anyone can have their own belief about spirituality. Some can even reject it, spirituality is connected with your emotions and soul, and directly and indirectly with the mind.

The Soul

Soul the most complex thing inside a human body, trapped inside the heart. A soul is a whole new different entity inside your body. Our body decays, your physical heart will decay, our minds will decay but how can the soul decay? A soul is the only human element or lets me rephrase it. A soul is one of the only living things that are eternal. It does migrate through different universes, and in the process, it does face the obstacles of death. And with every new life, the memory of the past becomes invisible. And unlike your body, your soul doesn't perish away but rather pass away to the other universe. Created, way before even our forefathers were born, a soul is a mystery. The soul is like the electricity in your house, careless of all the wirings and connections. If the current isn't passed through it, it will be empty and pointless. Our body is the wiring and soul, the current.

The soul is such a mystery that Allah SWT says, "And they ask you [O Muhammad] concerning the rooh [the spirit]. Say: 'The rooh: it is one of the things, the knowledge of which is only with my Lord. And of knowledge, you (mankind) have been given only a little.' [Quran, Surah al-Israa 17:85]"

Anyhow, you might wonder Billal what does the soul have to do with the context of this book? Well, my friend the "soul" would connect to everything I said earlier, directly and indirectly. From emotional to practical life and most importantly the "consciousness" that the book has been preaching throughout.

In this world, your soul is the only substance that has been the closest to Almighty and the heavens practically. Ever thought why we all desired a love that lasts or we all desperate for a "happy" life?

From the limited understanding I have, here is a theory. Soul after being altered to so many dimensions, having memory disorder and craving for the life of the eternal. The divine wisdom, I can think of regarding the soul could be, to push you near to the divine in order to eventually satisfy the need.

Let me put in simpler words, so your soul, being so fascinated by the glimpse of heaven it felt, comes to the other world, this world with his memory lost. But the need stayed with it. Now a divine reason, I can think of that happening is to bring you closer to your lord with the appetite of your soul.

Eventually, it becomes a fight of the desire of the soul versus the desire of the mind. The mind desires this world, the soul desires the next world. The mind has the evidence to show how beautiful the cars are and how pretty the creations are. The soul despite the glimpse has nothing to show or tell. That's why we eventually see, this world winning over the next one.

If you remember, from the start of the chapter of

emotions on what I said about humans, they are greedy, anxious, and short-sighted. We as humans are created lusty, trying to be clever, lost in our own doom.

Ever wondered why we crave a life that's free from good-byes. How we always want to be happy and hold on to people and things we have forever. This is why we desire a love that lasts, and life that stays. How we want to live a life, away from the worries of the world. How we want

With all the methods we try to prevent ourselves from growing into our graves. All the aging creams to serums. Now that we think about it, life is, when it's eternal. Life, what's the point of making all this money when you can't even spend it.

The Naafs

As I said the soul is naive, while the pious side works on a thought which is to be believed but not as yet seen. The cunning evil side, supported by the Shaitan himself, shows a person the greenery of this world. Your desires are directly inclined with your naafs. This concept here might be a spiritual one. But it has, it's rooted in everything in every single aspect of our lives that are associated with desires and pleasures. From drinking chocolate milk to consuming inappropriate content, every physical or mental desire is backed up, by the voice inside your head, to do it. Do it, it's alright. No one's seeing you. Do it, because everyone does it. To that extent when a person starts to get fooled by the truth itself. For example; "Do it, because your Lord is all-merciful".

Ever wondered why,

"Allah has set a seal upon their hearts and upon their hearing, and over their vision is a veil. And for them is a great punishment" (2-7)

The seal starts with obeying the desires, the seal ends with enslaving yourself to them. It's not like the person becomes blind or loses the power of hearing. It's just their hearts become trapped, in the walls of misguidance, arrogance, and ego. All they see his desire. All they do is, fulfill is desires.

They lose the ability to fight, control, and detach. We all are sinners, we all will sin. It's not the deed, but how you react to it afterward. Think about it, all the major sins are done with the lust of desire. From Alcohol to adultery. From murder to shirk and that's the highest possible result, but it gets uglier and worst every time.

If my friend, you truly want to be certain in the population of uncertain. And with that, I will introduce you to a concept I have been thinking about.

You might have heard about intelligent, emotional intelligence. There is another type of intelligence, most of us are unaware of.

The Spiritual Intelligence

While reading the philosophy of Al-Ghazli (r), he said something really interesting. So he talks about intellect, now we nowadays see it as more of a cognitive process, like chemistry or maths. But he says, the aqal (intellect) the real intellect restrains the soul from caprice/mood swings. And that's the real role of Aqal.

Intellect is the merciful partner of the soul, whereas the desires are the clear enemy. As Ghazali writes, a person has further four entities inside him. I will just talk about the main two, the shaitan and the angel. The shaitan influences the naafs, and the angel tries to stop the soul with the help of intellect.

Anyhow, coming back to the context, have you ever felt sad for like literally no reason at all? Like you, reflect on your day and your surroundings there nothing that went "wrong" then why? Similarly, ever took a nap in the evening and woke up all sad and lonely? A soul does feel burdens, have you ever thought why? Like why does the heart feel burdened? Why do we get hurt? Why do we get depressed, why do we become hopeless?

Maybe, it's the soul hinting to you and exposing to you the reality of life. And asking you to turn back to Allah. As there is an angel inside you supported by spiritual intelligence? Which wants you to wake up from a dark delusion.

Think about it, Oh you having a good time, having fun and all, and all of a sudden you get low. Why does that happen? Maybe that's the soul hinting, to turn to Allah. You all of a sudden get burdened about something. Oh, you're having a bad time? Turn to Allah. Maybe, all the troubles you face and all the tensions you have are a way for your soul to convey to you, To turn to Allah. No, not the psychiatrist. Allah, turn to Allah for peace.

You get depressed, after having such a nice weekend. Feeling all lonely and down, why? Maybe you were getting too much into the life of this world and you get struck by the reality from the spiritual intelligence to get back to God before it's too late.

Not just that, it's the spiritual intelligence that truly shows a person how fragile and vulnerable a person is without having Allah in their lives. Just like a leaf, blown away with the wind.

Escapism

From sleep, to meditation, from a good read to a soulful music session. We all need breaks, from work, relationships and even habits. Ever wonder, why? Why we need to breaks, why we get exhausted while doing something we usually love? It's the soul that gets tired of the noice and greed around. Escape, is a very beautiful element of spiritual life, we often see in our practical lives as well. It helps not only the soul but the mind to rethink, refresh and calms the soul. The world is like a heavy duty drug for the soul and escape is the repercussions. A soul needs its space from the noice and distractions of the world that escape can be a depression to you, but in reality it's the soul distancing itself from the materialistic world. The soul isn't natural or entirely comfortable with worldy greed and impurities.

Heart

The soul is mainly preserved in the heart, there are two types of heart, a physical heart, and a spiritual heart. The physical heart is the one, we are told to follow and stuff. The spiritual heart, which is also known as "Qalb" is like a mirror, the more you shine, away from the dirt of pleasure and desires. It shines more and reflects upon the soul the light, filled with peace and calmness. That light can be also known as the "noor" (the divine light), we often look at it on the face, but it's truly carried in the hearts.

Similarly, spiritual intelligence comes into every situation of life. Comfort in life is the byproduct of desires. In order to be unbreakable, you need to become friends with discomfort.

As through discomfort, you will find the importance of patience, you will understand why Allah loves patience and the patient so much. The lust of the mind never stops.

Well of desire can never be filled, it's through pain, discomfort, and patience. One truly finds their peace, their Lord and their true self.

It's Allah himself that wants you to escape the

prison of your mind, through hardships and pain. For example, waking up at 5 in the morning and doing ablution in the cold winters. Likewise, to fast 18 hours a day, in the hottest of summers. Why does Allah make all this obligatory for us?

We all know Allah does not need it, we know it so well we use it as an excuse. But, why does Allah want the body to go through difficulties in order to defeat the ego of the brain?

For me, life found new meanings and wisdom when I mixed Ghazali with Will Durant. When I understood the mind but didn't ignore the soul. For me, the true answers (I am still in pursuit of them) but were, when I all self-help over the base and roots of spiritualism.

"It's the intellect which is the light of the soul which shines in the mind"

"To become the certain in uncertain, we need to find comfort in discomfort"

FINAL THOUGHTS

I don't know, my friend if you even are reading this or not. But as the narrator, this book has struck me really hard. Writing a book has truly been a wonderful journey for me. I had the intent to write a book for a long time now. Just never got the right idea, the right concept that would not only be relatable to the reader but bring value in many aspects of life to my buddy reading the book.

I hope you find my work worth the value and I hope, I bring some bit of value to your emotional, spiritual and practical life.

Just always remember, **hopelessness is the lust of the weak.**

It technically may just have taken me a month or so to write this work, but it has a whole journey and life to it. It has my struggle of the last three years while learning, observing, and understanding. The behaviors, the patterns, some of the psychology and a lot of spiritualism.

I tried my best to cover as many bases and subjects as possible while staying relevant and well formatted and true to the context of the book. I DID

NOT focus a lot, on the vocabulary or the literature and grammar part of the book. It would be a blessing if you could not find any typos or poor grammar in almost every paragraph, if you found them. Please be easy on them and focus on what I am trying to say, rather how I say it. Also, it isn't a novel. Well, it wasn't intended to be.

There were a lot of topics, I wanted to cover but I couldn't. There were a lot of topics I wanted to cover more briefly, there were quite a few topics covered indirectly and there were a few obvious principals repeated constantly. I hope you understood the core perspective, I was trying to deliver rather than the topics. And with newer editions, I will try adding more and more value.

I compiled this book, from the reader's perspective. As I am a reader myself. I was one of the biggest critiques of my work. Deleted paragraphs on paragraphs, in order to keep it readable and relevant. And to be very frank, I would like to appreciate all the writers of any sort, as knowing something and writing it down, are two very different jobs. It was definitely not an easy job, but one that was worth it.

I hope this book strikes you as hard as it struck

me. And I really hope the book inspires a new lot of readers and writers. As I feel the art of writing a book is dying into smaller pieces of content, and I wish to inspire the bloggers into authors.

Everything I said or wrote in the book, might not be 100% applicable to you as well as might not be 100% relatable to you. As while I am focusing on each and every one of you, I am also targeting a whole mass. And don't forget the rule of expectation does exist and when you target a whole group of population, it's kind of difficult to address each and every issue ever.

One other very important thing I learned from my relatively short book was, as a reader, you never get satisfied with your work. Also, you just cannot put everything you know in your book, you need to stay true to the topic. And lastly, there will be always room for improvement but in order to grow, you have the courage to let it out there and improve.

Already working on two more very special and powerful books. As I am not just an author but a visionary and I want to target generations with my work. Inspire generations to growth, peace and unity. In this world run by behind the scene developments, with visions bigger than any other.

How to become certain in uncertain?

Achieving certainty is a whole process, starting from adapting to certain situations to changing the mindset in order to gain some consciousness. Have perspective, hope and courage.

To know more about me, you can read the next page. If not interested, then **THIS IS ALL FOLKS**

Oh and by the way, the educational system and the society, I am coming for you next.

Do share your thoughts on your social media or my website. Would love to hear from you. Feel free to text me, I will surely reply to you, my friend. # teamcertain

And a special thanks to everyone who supported me in this journey, Amena, Anam, Ahmed, Ghamama, Hassan, Moaz, Souman, Shakib, Umer and Zerfishan

ABOUT ME

In the last year of my teenage, I have always been keen to observe life and it's living from a deeper perspective. Someone who is highly influenced by the spiritual essence of life and growth.

I have never been someone with a very fancy portfolio, a high achiever, or the sweetheart of my circle. But one thing I was blessed with was the art of experimenting. From selling lemonade in the hot July of Lahore at the age of seven. To writing, a short story compilation book at the same age, to coding a calculator on a notepad at the age of thirteen. Everything I have done in my life, from writing a book to hosting a podcast, I have done it without the help of the system.

As always been underestimated and undermined, I developed the skill of redemption. Not holding onto any grudges or anything but redemption and inspiration to all those who think they cannot do it. Something I am really glad I had from a very young age was the power of taking challenges and the ability to take failures.

With appreciation for my past, to my past. At this moment, I am a Dreamer, Observer, and Analyst. I would observe the different whys and hows of human behavior and further share my opinion on them.

A Content Creator, A Podcaster, A Storyteller and A Certified Certainty and Purpose Coach, aspiring inspirational speaker, a hustling entrepreneur since the age of seven. And now, most recently, A Writer.

One thing, I was most certainly from a very age was to not limit myself to one job, one profession, or one skill. I was never the type of person, who was ready to accept himself as a bank manager and die as the area manager or a head city manager with all due respect. With blessgings and Guidance from Allah, this would not be the last time you hear from me.

Social Media handles: @iambillal

For any query, you can email me at <u>me@iambillal.com</u> and visit my website for blogs, podcasts and content.

FOR PERSONAL NOTES:

TO BE FILLED BY THE AUTHOR WHEN WE MEET: